PLAY LEFT FULLBACK

How **Challenging the Status Quo** Will
Help America's Solo and Small Firm
Lawyers Build Better Practices, Be
Heroes to their Families, and **Restore
America's Trust in Lawyers**

BEN GLASS

www.amplifypublishing.com

Play Left Fullback

For more information, please contact:
Mascot Books
620 Herndon Parkway #320
Herndon, VA 20170
info@mascotbooks.com

Library of Congress Control Number: 2019911502

CPSIA Code: PRFRE1219A
ISBN-13: 978-1-64307-472-6

Printed in Canada

As you will see when you read this book, I have been fortunate to have a handful of people come into my life who have had a profound impact on where I find myself today.

This book is dedicated to three of them: my mom, my dad, and my wife.

Mom and Dad, you raised all seven of your children in a loving environment and you taught us to use our gifts wisely; always say "please," "thank-you," and "yes sir/yes ma'am," and to ask "how can I help you?" first. These were simple yet enduring lessons. No one could go wrong by following your examples for living.

Sandi, we were so young when we met and got married, and yet "not knowing what we didn't know," we have not only survived but thrived in the ups and downs of an extremely busy and interesting life together. Our children and I have benefitted greatly from your example for living.

Thank you all.

Ben

FREE REPORTS, VIDEOS, AND MORE ARE READY FOR YOU

Would you like to see what goes into growing a solo/small law firm?

Want the latest information on online marketing, print advertisements, direct mail, broadcast ads, and more?

How about seeing "inside the mind" of how I grew and continue to grow my law firm?

I'll give you an insider's look at the process when you request my latest free offer at:

www.GreatLegalMarketing.com

Fair warning: I offer an unvarnished take on what it means to operate your law firm as a business. It doesn't always line up with the stuff you hear from the routine sources that speak to lawyers like you and me. But I promise you, it will give you both the ideas and sense of permission needed to finally grow your practice into the business you really want it to be.

CONTENTS

A DISCLAIMER
ACTUALLY WORTH READING

This book is about your life. It has a lot of advice for living, but it is not intended to be legal or ethical advice. Legal requirements and ethical standards governing client relationships, marketing, and duties to clients vary from state to state. If you didn't already know it, only you are responsible for your own actions. This is a major theme of this book.

Neither the author nor the publisher makes any warranties, express or implied, about whether any of the material or instructions in this book are legally or ethically appropriate in your jurisdiction. To the extent that you disagree with my views on what we lawyers should be doing with our lives and our practices—write your own book and put it out into the world as I have done. If you do write such a book, I will read it.

This book can make you rich in many ways, but I make no income representations. Many lawyers who have been exposed to the ideas in this book end up taking action and reaping financial, emotional, and professional benefits. On the other hand, some will buy this book but never crack the cover. Whether you will survive and thrive in a world of cutthroat competition, ruthless marketing vultures, 800-pound gorillas, and a new consumer-driven economy for legal services depends entirely on your proclivity to take action, manage yourself and others, establish priorities, and provide competent legal services.

Finally, while my editor wanted to insist that I write his/her or switch up the use of he/she every time I needed to use a gender-specific pronoun, I refuse. It looks silly and would not change the importance of this book one bit. This book is obviously meant for everyone.

INTRODUCTION
THE ELITE ARE WRONG!

The answer to the "lawyer wellness" problem is not "mindfulness meditation," the creation of "wellness" programs, or more mandatory continuing legal education.

The answer is **build a real business.**

I f you've watched me at all over the last decade, you can tell that I really don't care all that much about what the bar, as a whole, does. I care deeply about my own family, the legacy I am leaving, my employees, and my clients (in that order).

Everyone has to make their own decisions about what matters. I know that I have positively influenced, on both the business and the family side, more solo and small firm lawyers than any other "guru" out there. This is a part of my legacy.

I know that I am not for everyone. I am not interested in being the "biggest" or having trained "the most." If all you want to know about is how to get and convert more leads, I can point you to a dozen companies that actually do that pretty well. Most run seminars to get you to buy their marketing services, but that might be exactly what you need. If you are comfortable getting your practice-building advice from people who are not actually lawyers, I can give you a list of coaches to choose from. Again, it's fine to get your advice there if you are going in with eyes open.

If it doesn't bother you to get "how to build a better life with your law practice" advice from people whose personal lives are a wreck, have at it.

I do what interests me, and what interests me is working with lawyers who "get it." It's time for lawyers to re-prioritize their lives. You've worked hard to get where you are and it's time to reap the rewards.

In 2016, the National Task Force on Lawyer Well-Being published a report on "lawyer wellness." Subtitled, Creating a Movement to Improve Well-Being in the Legal Profession, the findings of the report were ugly. Turns out that many lawyers are not all that satisfied with the path they have chosen as their life's work. Some find that the pressures of being a lawyer in today's ultra-competitive, hyper-fast, consumer-driven environment are so challenging that, overworked and underpaid, they become anxious and depressed, then turn to drugs and alcohol and other self-harming behaviors, including suicide, to escape the pressure. Sadly, younger lawyers tend to be more likely to be adversely affected by the supposed "norms" of the profession.

This is not good for clients or society as these lawyers will often find themselves burned out, the subject of bar complaints and malpractice suits. At the very least, the advice they give and the work they do will not be their best. How can you be the creative lawyer that society needs when you are in financial and personal distress?

Lawyer unhappiness is bad for families, too. Sixty-hour workweeks, missed soccer games and piano recitals, and a spouse who is left wondering, "Will this ever get better?" will suck the life right out of your entire family.

Even those who do not totally flame out, destroying themselves and the lives around them, will often wake up asking themselves, "Is that all there is? Did I really work as hard as I did in school and in my career up to now for *this?*"

Many in the legal profession expressed surprise at the findings of the National Task Force report. The Committee on Lawyer Well-Being in Virginia (where I practice) said in its "Profession at Risk" report that the data in the report, "Sent shockwaves through the American legal community." State Bar journals across the country exploded with "it's time to change" articles from State Bar presidents.

While the Task Force report may have come as a surprise to those in ivory towers, anyone who is actually in the trenches meeting clients, trying cases, attending hearings, taking depositions, and yes, hanging out with other lawyers at professional and social events knows that many lawyers live lives of abject misery. Endless worry and uncertainty about where the next client is coming from, disappointed spouses and kids, together with out-of-control client demands and poor time management drive lawyer unhappiness.

Life *is* really stressful when you feel like you have worked very hard to get where you are yet don't make enough money; don't have enough time to enjoy the money you make; aren't representing people you like to represent doing the work you enjoy most; and aren't working with business partners, associates, and employees you like to work with.

That life sucks.

But the "answer" from the National Task Force, the American Bar Association, and every state bar that has attempted to address the problem of lawyer "unwellness" is wrong. Every state that has formed a committee to study or published proposed solutions to the issue has arrived at this general list of "solutions" to the problem:

1. Emphasize that well-being is part of a lawyer's duty of competence and a top priority for the profession, as though we didn't already know this.

2. Spend money (typically by increasing the mandatory dues that lawyers already pay) and appoint (more) committees to explore, "health and wellness initiatives, including meditation classes."

3. Provide more funding (again, funded by increases in mandatory dues) for those state-wide organizations which provide assistance to lawyers who need behavioral and health assistance services.

4. Create Continuing Legal Education (CLE) courses, and, in some cases, *require* lawyers to attend courses on "professional health initiatives," whatever that means.

What the ABA and the Rest of the Elite Still Don't Get

These answers will never be sufficient to solve the problem!

Here's what over thirteen years of coaching—through live events, webinars, books, newsletters, and one-on-one sessions—thousands of solo and small firm lawyers around the United States has demonstrated without question:

> *Teaching lawyers how to build a better business—one that serves their families, their clients, and the community—should be the TOP PRIORITY for everyone involved in the profession. The real shock about the National Task*

Force report is not that lawyers are in distress—it's that no one who has looked at the issue has even suggested that building a better business is a crucial ingredient for lawyer wellness.

As long as the established bar continues to refuse to acknowledge that the skills that make one a good lawyer are not the skills that allow one to grow a profitable and fun business, *and that both are necessary* if lawyers are truly to be "well," we will continue to try to fix major hemorrhaging with Band-Aids. The patients will continue to get sick and die.

We are spending time on the wrong issues. Let me give you an example:

In my home state of Virginia, we are required to attend twelve hours of mandatory Continuing Legal Education every year. That requirement does not mandate that we do anything other than show up (or attend an online video). It's like getting a participation trophy. No one's checking that lawyers are *learning* anything that might actually be useful to a client because there's no requirement that (1) the classes we attend be applicable to our practice area, and (2) that we actually have listened and absorbed. Even though there is not a shred of evidence that mandatory CLE makes the lawyers in Virginia any better than, say, Maryland lawyers, where CLE is not required, the requirement will never go away because, according to a footnote buried deep in an appendix to Virginia's Lawyer Well-being report, the Virginia State Bar collects over $500,000 in CLE *late fees* alone. Incredible.

You know what the Virginia State Bar doesn't think you should learn about?

Yes, that's right—running a great business. One that makes you and your family rich.

Here's a partial list of vitally important education you cannot get CLE credit for in Virginia:

1. Marketing, business development, and sales training

2. Client development methods and strategies

3. Enhancing profits

4. Strategic business planning

5. Improving cash reserves

6. Employee morale and motivation

7. Hiring and retention

Sorry, but you can't run a business unless you are highly skilled in each of these areas. These topics should actually be a top priority for all of us, but especially for the solo and small firm market in which you and I live.[1]

The fact that the bar finds these topics "just not worth the time" should not stop you from living your life and choosing to get better at them because you will be happier and richer when you master them. A great lawyer who doesn't know how to get clients, produce a profit, and hire and manage a staff (all while *Still Getting Home in Time for Dinner*, the subtitle of my first book for lawyers) is useless.

---

1. In May, 2019, the Virginia State Bar's Special Committee on Lawyer Well-Being published a report on *The Occupational Risks of the Practice of Law*. The report made many good recommendations for improving lawyers' lives, much of which is already included in the Great Legal Marketing curriculum. Among other things, the report recognized that business management, accounting, marketing, finance, and technology are vitally important skills, especially to solo and small firm attorneys. Sadly, the report did not make a recommendation that education in these areas also qualify for "lawyer wellness" continuing legal education credit.

Useless to himself because he will always be stressing about the next client;

Useless to his family because he will never be there for them;

Useless to his clients because he can't do his best work when stressed to the max;

Useless to society because there will be no time for pro bono work; and,

Useless because he is much more likely to burn out, turn to substances for relief, and cheat on his clients.

But an average lawyer who figures out how to run a business that serves him and his family, that produces enough profit to hire great staff who can deliver not only quality legal care but terrific customer service—now *that* lawyer will be a hero to his family and an icon in the community.

Isn't that what we want?

So I have an invitation for you:

If you're searching for a more balanced alternative, a happier home, a healthier lifestyle, and a more holistic way to live your life and build your practice, so that you can be both *hero* and *icon*, then what you're doing at this very minute is precisely what you *should* be doing: holding this book in your hand.

I'm also inviting you to do something else—and for many of you, it will require a significant shift in your philosophy and a bold break from your previous way of thinking.

Let's decide to break free of the narrow mindset of the traditional legal establishment. The established bar has not taken a real leadership position on this issue, perhaps because they didn't think it was actually possible, but more likely because they don't live where you and I live. On the ground. In the trenches. Every day.

It's okay. I'll lead.

Every concept that I put forward in this book, every challenge, new idea, and new way of thinking that you'll read here flies directly in the face of what you have been taught about how lawyers should view the profession and their roles in it . . . and with good reason.

The old way of looking at our profession is killing us and *they* have no good answers for us. But that's not really *their* job, is it? It's *your* job to map out your life, first.

What I really want you to challenge is the pervasive, outdated notion amongst the legal traditionalists that your sacrifice, suffering and self-abuse are prerequisites for success and enjoyment in the law; that putting service before all else is necessary and even noble, and that combining "profit" with "law firm" in the same sentence is evil.

This stuff is nonsense. And it's also, well, *dumb*. Destructive. Dangerously short-sighted, and, yes, even potentially fatal. This is your life we are talking about. The world owes you nothing despite the hard work you put in to get your law degree but, importantly, you don't owe the world anything, either. Stop listening to them.

For too long now too many good, solid human beings have burned out of a profession that should be a source of joy. Hell, we *help* people.

As the Task Force report makes clear, many others are teetering on disaster, one step away from burn-out, emotional and financial bankruptcy, or worse.

Striving to be a great lawyer with a thriving practice, a strong brand, and a healthy, well-balanced life, working with clients and staff that you like, should be the norm, not an anomaly. It is not only an attainable goal but, in my view, a necessity.

Here's the real problem: the reason we have lawyer wellness committees, forums, and seminars is that for far too long the profession has been looking inward for ideas. Lawyers have been slow

to innovate, modernize, and adapt to the changing needs of consumers. Further, we have been slowed by a regulatory regime that
is, in large part, not good for lawyers or consumers. Look around.
Lawyers are no longer the only go-to source for legal services. If
you don't know how to (or aren't allowed to) build what consumers
actually want, you will be dead in the water, guaranteed.

If you are a solo or small firm attorney, *you should be the hero
of your family and community.* You are a superior being who should
be acknowledged and thanked because you are not only ensuring
that legal services across the entire legal spectrum are available to
everyone, but you are doing it while taking on one of the biggest
challenges in our society: running a small business.

It is YOU—the solo and small firm lawyers—that I not only
want to thank but also want to invite to crack open this book to
learn more about the essential elements of living (and lawyering)
that some say have been deliberately kept from you by the traditional legal establishment.

I'll say it now, loud and clear:

There is another way to live, a better way to prosper and grow,
and a saner, more civilized way to build your practice and live a life
of significance and meaning.

You deserve to look at your life and your law practice (in that
order of priority) through a different lens, a wider lens, a more
all-encompassing lens that will expand your vision and help you
become brave enough to **put you and your family first**, perhaps for
the first time in your legal career.

Getting your priorities right is the source from which everything else will flow—more clients getting their problems solved,
stronger balance sheets, greater productivity, a happier home life,
fewer problems with drug and alcohol abuse, et cetera. This is
how your growth and prosperity will unfold—not by a very nar-

row-minded approach to what it means to "be a lawyer."

It's time now for **renegade thinking**: outside forces are reshaping the whole concept of what it means to be a lawyer. Consumers are in charge. Those who continue to view the legal experience through the lawyer's eyes, and not the consumer's eyes, will not enjoy their future. Lawyers may have originally structured the law, but consumers don't care about tradition. They just want their problems solved.

So this is an important theme of the book, and a concept that I hit pretty hard with my attorney members: you deserve to put your family and your family's well-being, health, and financial security ahead of all else—and to do it boldly, without apology, without fear, and without doubt. You have worked hard and sacrificed much for this.

Don't misunderstand: the concept of service is laudable. Frankly, I don't know any lawyer who does not already go "above and beyond" in this regard. But unless and until you build your business *first*, unless and until you put what makes you happy at the top of your priority list, you will continue to live a life that is not fulfilled.

I'm sure that you were taught in law school that *the law is a learned profession*, but Eric Hoffer had it right:

> *"In times of change, learners will inherit the earth while the learned find themselves beautifully equipped to deal with a world that no longer exists."*

Okay, I'm listening, but why listen to anything at all that Ben Glass has to say on this subject?

My life is very good. I run two highly profitable businesses; am very happily married to my best friend, Sandi, since 1981; have nine children (four adopted from China); and also five grandchildren. As this book is being released I have sent seven kids off to six different Virginia universities. I come and go from my businesses as I please, get to referee highly competitive youth and high school soccer teams, and participate in CrossFit®. I provide jobs, financial security, and a great place to work for about sixteen people, and I get invited to speak to lawyers and entrepreneurs all over the country. My law firm is thriving and successful (check out Ben-GlassLaw.com and JustReadTheReviews.com).

In short, I am free to live my life as I want.

I am also the only full-time, practicing lawyer in the nation who is leading a tribe of thousands of lawyers who are comfortable with the notion that it's okay to have fun and make good money in the practice of law. They have reimagined what it means to "practice law" in their communities.

I'm pretty confident that my law clients *and* the growing membership of Great Legal Marketing are all grateful for the services I provide and the knowledge that I share—and I consider myself blessed to be able to do it.

But don't just listen to my voice. Listen to theirs:

"Since becoming a member of Great Legal Marketing, our receivables have more than doubled in less than three years! It's brought our family closer together due to the fewer hours I have to work. My husband was even able to quit his job to come work for the firm!"
—Michele Lewane,
Worker's Compensation Lawyer, Virginia

. . .

"After seventeen years in private practice, a deployment to Iraq as an Army lawyer created a 'tactical pause' in my

life. In search of the best way to start over, I discovered Ben Glass. Great Legal Marketing soon transformed my old way of lawyering into a new way of thinking, acting, and now growing as a business."

—Tim George,
Personal Injury Lawyer, Pennsylvania

. . .

"Ben's presentation of sensible, realistic goals and ideas works. Period. I've personally reduced my commute by two hours and twenty-five minutes. I attend all of my children's sporting events and activities. I've increased profits and caseload; and—oh yeah—I really enjoy what I am doing again, thanks to the ideas and encouragement you'll find here."

—Brian Mittman,
Social Security Disability Lawyer, New York

This is only a tiny sampling of the thousands of emails, letters, and testimonials I receive from lawyers all over the country who have learned how to look at themselves and their practices differently.

A Brief Word About Gurus and Charlatans

I know that each day your email inbox is filled with "How to get more leads and improve your practice" spam, almost all of it put out there by individuals who have never met with a law client; suffered through an adverse jury verdict; actually run a profitable law firm (or business of any kind) on their own; and who have no idea of the conversations you and your spouse have late at night about the pressures you face. I do.

The reason your email box is filled is because *they* see you as an easy mark. They know that most lawyers are undertrained in marketing, sales, and the running of a business, and they prey on that. You can thank the law schools and the established bar for that. Remember, though, that Google is your friend here. Before you get involved with the "guru of the week," Google them. Better yet, reach out to me.

I'm here to fill that gap and to lead.

Now let's let the real work begin.

Benjamin W. Glass, III
October 1, 2019

SECTION I

BECOMING BEN: THE BACKSTORY

CHAPTER ONE
NOTHING FRAGILE ABOUT *THIS* GLASS HOUSE!
AMERICANA IN ANNANDALE, VIRGINIA

We Begin in My Backyard

We had the flattest backyard in the neighborhood.

Looking back on it now, I'm pretty sure it was our flat backyard—one of many things, of course—that helped push me towards success. Thank God for our flat backyard.

It made our house a magnet.

I grew up in a close-knit community in Annandale, Virginia, where kids—and plenty of them, too—ran freely from house to house, families left their front doors unlocked, and the only thing you had to worry about when it started getting dark was to remember to hightail it home for dinner before the streetlights came on.

And if the streetlights weren't enough of a reminder that it was almost time for dinner (and yes, those were the days when mothers served dinner to their families and fathers pulled into their driveways from a long day of work just in time to eat), you didn't really need to worry: my mother had a cowbell.

She'd always been a brilliant woman, but it didn't dawn on me until much later in my life just how brilliant she really was. And not just brilliant, but *efficient*: with seven kids who were usually spread out all over the neighborhood when dinner was about to go onto the table, clanging a cowbell was much more efficient than going from house to house searching for her clan or hollering out the window to call us home. She wouldn't have done either, I'm sure. With seven children, she was a busy woman.

Mom was busy in the busiest sense of the word, keeping us in line, washing our clothes, cooking meals, volunteering at school, cooking more meals, meeting with our teachers, and taking us to church. Oh, and did I say cooking our meals? When dinner was ready, it was time to eat—as simple as that. Mom was not going to be bothered with a house-to-house search or a clarion call for her kids to come home to eat.

No, the cowbell was best.

And did we ever come running! As the oldest of us seven, I kind of saw it as my responsibility to help keep things in order, to help keep things running smoothly, to make sure we were all where we needed to be when Mom needed us to be there, especially when Dad was still at work. (My brothers and sisters would no doubt disagree with my description of "keeping things in order." They would describe what I did as "being bossy.")

I took these responsibilities seriously, too, not because Mom ever came out and asked me to, but because I knew it needed to be done—and as the oldest, I was the one to do it. (Much later, when

I played on a national champion youth soccer team, I was the des-
ignated penalty kicker. Everyone else, good as they were, were unwilling to shoulder that burden.)

I'm sure it was my need for establishing (and maintaining) a
sense of order in the midst of all of that happy family chaos that
helped develop my leadership abilities, which carried over into my
adult life, of course.

Plus, being around a lot of other kids—whether it was the kids
in my neighborhood (there must have been about thirty of us kids
within ten houses of each other at any given time) or just my other
six siblings—was, well, it was just *fun*, plain and simple.

It gave me the feeling that I was connected to something
larger than just myself. I still remember how *good* it felt—that
sense of belonging, that sense of purpose, that sense of place. It
was a safe place.

I feel very blessed to enjoy all of very same feelings today,
with my own wife and children. They give me that same sense
of belonging, purpose, and place—and the good news is that my
siblings are all friends. We still live close to each other. Our links
have never been broken. This family stuff is what helps give my
life meaning and sustainability. *This* is what I have identified as
my top priority.

So looking back, I realize how deeply we all really loved each
other. But equally important, we all *liked* each other.

We still do.

．．．

When I look back on the days of my youth, I remember just
really enjoying all of the constant *movement and motion* that was us.
I loved the noisiness and the crowd. Hey, I even enjoyed sharing a
bedroom with my younger brothers Daniel and Thomas.

It's not only safe but it's accurate to say that all of the values I grew up with as a kid—the importance of collective responsibility, accountability, hard work, *teamwork*—helped mold me into the successful lawyer, leader, business owner, father, and husband that I am today.

In fact, it is these very values, and the importance of knowing how to prioritize what's most important in life (with my top priority being the financial well-being and emotional security of my family) that stand at the center of what I teach to today's solo and small firm lawyers: get clear in your own mind what you want your life to be and then figure out the type of practice that serves that life and the type of client that serves that practice. Then create marketing for *that* client.

Though I'll go into deeper detail later on in the book, knowing how to attract and make happy your *avatar* client is the most effective tool a lawyer has in his toolbox—and getting crystal clear about what you want for your life is really the *only* way to attract the right kind of new clients, grow your business, and survive in a world that's filled with competitive, cutthroat marketing vultures and thousands of other attorneys out there who are equally desperate to distinguish themselves from the pack. In order to be "well" as an attorney your business skills must trump your lawyer skills. Being the best lawyer in town is no advantage in the marketplace because the consumer has no way of knowing who is "best."

Here are three important questions. You should be crystal clear about the answers:

What kind of life do I want to be living? What role do I play in making sure that this life becomes a reality for me? What do I need to do next to create my own reality?

Once you've asked yourself those questions—and once you've decided on the answers—then you **build your law firm around** *that*. You must put a plan in place that ensures that you are continually working towards the life you want. To do otherwise is to be miserable. If you don't know what you want for (and from) your life, you are without a foundation—a ship without a rudder—and in this case, even the best marketing plan coupled with the best lawyer skills won't help you.

Here's the link I really want to make—the hook that links my backstory to my present-day life: I've always had a pretty clear understanding of the kind of life I've wanted to lead. I kind of knew from an early age because this is what my parents taught me, that *family was my first priority*—taking care of them, assuring their safety, both financial and emotional. What I didn't know was how to do that with a law firm. I missed that class in law school and the profession still doesn't teach it. Most lawyers are rather clueless about it. There aren't a whole lot of *good* books or seminars about it, either.

But I figured it out and I like sharing what I figure out with others. As the video at BenGlassLaw.com says, "Inspiring others is what I was born to do."

I guess that's why I've emerged as the foremost expert for solo and small firm lawyers in this field, and why so many thousands of lawyers turn to me and become members of Great Legal Marketing—to help them get to this sense of clarity and purpose about their lives, first, and then not mess it up by deciding to run a law firm.

So the long and short of it is this: My large, loving family really did play a vital role in the man I have become today. The Ben in my backstory is the Ben that lives and thrives within me to this very day. There is a direct link, a sustained connection, and I consider myself blessed to even have this awareness.

Someone asked me recently if there were any negative or dark memories that might have shaped the person I have become, and while there was certainly sadness, trauma, and unexpected setbacks, it was never sustained enough to have cast a shadow over my life. (We did lose *some* soccer games. We did *not* blame the referees.)

Sure, there were some dark moments. The occasional brawl here and the spontaneous shouting match there—after all, we were seven children living in a very small house.

But mostly, there was love.

Because we were so many of us, we became the sum of all of our parts. We were a single thing, made up from nine, separate things. And sure, we were as windblown and as fast-moving as a hurricane . . . but we belonged to each other, as a single entity, which helped us survive the storms, and Lord knows there were plenty that came our way.

Even though what I'm about to say next is really for a later chapter, I still want to introduce it here because it's an important part of my backstory: It was growing up in a large and loving family that made me want to have a large and loving family of my own, as an adult—which is exactly what I did when I met and married my beautiful wife and brilliant best friend, Sandi.

My point is this: Decide what's important to you in life. If you're blessed to have made that decision early on in your life, like I did, then consider yourself fortunate that you've been given a head start.

But even if you're still deciding—and if you're a young lawyer, there's a good chance that you're probably still trying to put this all together—realize that this is the most important decision you're ever going to make.

Sure, your priorities will shift from time to time, as you grow, as your family grows, as you transition from one stage to another—that's a given. What you need to keep in mind is that no matter what those priorities are, or how often they shift, you should always try to make sure that *you* make the decisions for *your own life*. No excuses. Stop listening to anyone who tries to guilt you into believing otherwise.

What I ask of the young lawyers and the new lawyers who are reading my book is this: Please, make these vital decisions—not just about your life but about your place in the world and about the kind of practice you want to have—first. Do that before you follow anyone's marketing strategies. My message to the more seasoned lawyers who are reading this is: it is never too late to grab the reins, take control, and live the life you were meant to live.

But back to the backyard.

Back to my dusty, beautiful backyard: I could understand how someone who is reading about "the Glass backyard" for the first time might want to visualize it as clean and clear as glass itself. I mean, after all, we're *talking* about a Glass backyard, right?

Well, think again.

In fact, move your mind to the entirely *opposite* end of the Glass backyard spectrum—because our backyard was not so much a sparkling, shimmering lake as it was, well, a *dust bowl*.

It was a dust bowl because it was the centerpiece and the star attraction for all neighborhood sports—so, much to my dad's chagrin, the sight of supple, green grass was never, *ever* a part of our reality.

There were too many of us underfoot, running like wild men at breakneck speed, chasing all types of balls and each other—and it wasn't just the kids in our family. This was the community field.

At least it was a dust bowl with purpose; a dust bowl that gave plenty of people plenty of pleasure. Four Division I college athletes came out of that backyard: me and my friends Steve (baseball) and Scott (football) Norwood and Mike Celec (soccer). Scott went on to a long career in the NFL.

So yes, I did try hard to keep my sisters and brothers in line whenever I could. I *did* try hard to pitch in and help my parents out when I had the time and the inclination . . . but if the "pitching" ever involved the throwing of a baseball, then let's face it: Mom was just flat out of luck, because that's where I would be, in the dust bowl, pitching fastballs, stealing bases, making tackles, scoring goals, rounding third with two men out, and sliding into home plate, sometimes all in the same afternoon.

So in a very real way, it was our back*yard* that really strengthened my back*story*. It was my dusty little backyard and the countless games of soccer, whiffle ball, baseball, kickball, and just about any other sport you can imagine, that first ignited my competitive spirit—even way back then.

Yes, it was a rough-and-tumble life, but there was also order in the midst of all the chaos, and there was love. Mom and Dad protected us at all costs—which is ironic, in a way, because we never really saw it as being protected. We saw it as being loved, because we didn't need to be protected. That wasn't the kind of world we lived in; not like the world we live in today, anyway.

Back in the '60s, we *survived* not wearing seatbelts. We *survived* bumping around in the back of our station wagon, bouncing around like little loose cannons. We survived eating processed foods and undercooked hamburger patties and white sugar and carb-loaded foods and very, very salty stuff. And, oh yes, we did walk a mile to school each way, unaccompanied by any adult.

We were *safe*—even though nobody locked their doors at night and every kid in the neighborhood roamed freely from house to house, even at night. We were safe, even though cars were left open all night, with the windows rolled down, on just about any street, anywhere, any time.

We were Americana in Annandale, and all that we had was enough.

All that we had was *more* than enough.

. . .

I realize, now, that it was growing up with this sense of belonging and security that gave me the roadmap I needed to lead my own nine children on this same journey.

Sandi and I have tried to raise our brood with that same love, that same dedication, and that same fierce commitment to live out our dreams—and we do everything we can to make sure we never lose sight of these priorities.

This is what we do. This is what my parents did.

This much I know for sure: I am blessed with a beautiful backstory. No, we weren't wealthy by any means and yes, we ate Mom's meatloaf more often than we ate steak.

But for this little boy, a dusty backyard, a clanging cowbell, and a large, loving family were the only things I ever really needed.

The Playground Lady and the Engineer

The Playground Lady

Both of my parents were very present in our lives; they were present in the lives of all seven of their children. Equally important—and this wasn't always the case with the parents of a large brood, especially in that day and time, back in the '60s and early '70s—they were present for *each other*.

My mom might have been busy making sure that the Glass household ran as efficiently and as smoothly as a family of nine could possibly run—an extraordinary feat in and of itself—but she also placed a high priority on our education, our health, and our religious upbringing.

Looking back on it now, I guess the best way to describe her would be in one word: *Supermom*. On any given day, with any one of her seven children, she could be found at school or volunteering in the classroom. Or, maybe chaperoning a field trip or playing the role of "room mother." (Do they even still have those?) Or, one of her favorites, helping out on the playground.

She seemed to be everywhere at once, and always present when we needed her—*whenever* we needed her. Even to this day, when I'm talking about her or remembering how much of a vital, visible role she played in our lives, I think of her as *the model of what moms strive to be*: Present. Hard-working. Loving. Firm when she had to be. And the best playground lady a little boy could have ever asked for.

But it was more than her presence on the playground. It was more than her putting dinner on the table and being happy, even eager, to greet my father when he got home from work at about 5:30 every night.

I guess what struck me most, what had the most powerful and profound effect on me back then, and still does to this very day, was the fact that both she and Dad always, always made *us* their highest priority . . . and we knew it.

Sure, Dad was the breadwinner and the enforcer and, when he had to be, the disciplinarian (though neither of them were ever that strict, simply because they didn't *need* to be). He played plenty of important roles in the family, as did Mom, but the most important, by a long shot?

Their role as our mentors, teaching us the values of being kind to others, working hard on our own stuff, having faith in God, and being forever learners. We were the center of their lives, and we knew it.

What was *most* important to them—more important than my father's job as an electrical engineer; more important than my mom's duties as a housewife, wife, and mother; even more important than the thousands of breakfasts, lunches, and dinners that Mom would place on our kitchen table day after day, night after night, year after year, was the steadfast belief—no, the steadfast *knowledge*—that we were the center of their universe. (Quick question: based on your activities this past week, would your kids say this about you?)

We were the dream that they worked so hard to realize; that they fought so hard to make come true.

And now that I've written it down, now that I've really reflected on it and transferred it from my long-ago memory to the form of these written words, I realize that everything they did, every move they made, defined and encapsulated the mindset that I now have and teach about the world in general and about life as a lawyer, specifically.

Why do I say this? Because both of my parents decided early on what kind of life they wanted to live and what priorities were most important to them—and every action they took, every decision they made, every goal they set, flowed from this awareness.

That's the very definition of "live life big."

Please, if you do nothing else with this book, commit to yourself and to your family. Too many lawyers voice a commitment to family without backing that commitment up with any action. My promise to you is that you can build a practice that serves all parts of your life.

Maybe that's why I'm so passionate about these concepts today—because they kind of flow through the blood in my veins and hang out in my very DNA. They've been a part of me since I've been a part of myself, since *before* the beginning.

I'm sure that's why so many thousands of lawyers—young and old, male and female, representing every consumer and small business legal discipline that exists—are members of Great Legal Marketing—because they know that the principles that I teach, I teach straight from real life, not from theory.

My mom was the master marketer. She certainly knew her "brand" (her family) and she knew exactly which tools were at her disposal to help get her message to her intended audience (her cowbell).

The master marketer, indeed.

A Note: *During the writing of this book my mom passed away after a long battle with pulmonary fibrosis. Over 320 people attended her funeral, held at St. Michael's Catholic Church in Annandale. That's pretty good for an eighty-four year old. Mom influenced a lot of people in her life, young and old, not by any lectures, but by the way she lived her life (she never met a stranger) and by the way she died: Dignified. Brave. Faithful. As my family reflected back on her life, we asked ourselves, "What was Mom's secret?" Here it is: when you were in her presence, she made you feel like you were the most important person in the world to her at that moment. She was always "present." Think about that for a moment.*

The Engineer

Even though Dad was a dedicated and brilliant electrical engineer and one of the smartest men I've ever known, I never, *ever* wanted him to help me with my homework—especially math!

None of us kids did.

I mean, if I was working on an algebra problem and I'd been struggling for a while with a particular equation, anybody else might have just given me the answer . . . but not Dad. No way.

Not only would he *not* give me the answer, but we'd have to go through the entire history and origin of the algebraic equation—*and* analyze how this particular problem might in some way have related to electrical engineering.

My father, Ben Glass, Jr., always seemed to be a blur of movement—but a solid, sturdy blur, if such a thing is possible. He worked every day and came home every night. He did help us with our homework, and he was always coaching one or more of us kids in some sport or another—usually soccer or basketball, on multiple teams at multiple times, because there were so many of us.

Dad was the one who eventually taught me geometry in a way that I understood it, in real-life terms: Through him, I learned about triangulation, adjacent angles, and transferal planes. He brought these geometric terms to life for me in a way that no geometry book ever could, and who would think I'd ever have to apply any of these principles out there in the real world?

I was just as surprised as anybody. Listen to this:

When Dad was our soccer coach, we were often required to go out onto the soccer fields that hadn't been marked—and most of the fields in Northern Virginia, at least back in those days, didn't have any markings. They were just dirt fields in the back of schools. So we had to do it ourselves, which meant creating a perfect one hundred-yard by sixty-yard rectangle. It's harder than it looks!

Being able to come to this task using the precision of geometric principles helped me tremendously. And it was Dad who taught me that precision; always lending his wisdom. (Thanks, Dad.)

Being an engineer at heart, Dad also obviously had a real knack for building and tinkering—and he was good at it, too. Each newborn sibling that Mom and Dad brought home from the hospital meant more rooms were needed in the house, so as the family grew, Dad just kept throwing up more walls in the basement and making more bedrooms!

No, he probably wasn't adhering to any local building codes, but Dad didn't care. Ben Glass, Jr., was not the kind of man who needed to ask for (or receive) anybody's permission. He was a bit of a renegade himself.

More than anything, though, it was the values of hard work, perseverance, and honesty that Dad instilled in all of us. When it came to living his life, Dad really walked the walk.

He didn't just *talk* about his dreams, he actualized them. Made them happen. Put plans and ideas into action and movement. Maybe that was because he was an engineer at heart, but I like to think it's also because of the fine and solid man that he was.

CHAPTER TWO
PLAY LEFT FULLBACK
(LESSONS FROM MY YOUTH)

I Can Get You That in a Size Ten

This might sound a little hard to believe, but I "dealt" out of my high school locker.

No, not drugs.

Sports equipment. Soccer stuff, to be exact.

I've already mentioned that sports—particularly soccer—was an important part of my life growing up. In the 1970s, Northern Virginia was one of the places in America where soccer first exploded into a national phenomenon. So it's not really that much of an exaggeration to say that soccer's meteoric rise in popularity kind of began right in my backyard (my dusty backyard), in Annandale, Virginia!

Because we were so athletic, we were also very competitive. Participating in competitive sports—again, particularly soccer—really ignited the flame of my competitive spirit; again, it was in my DNA.

Second entrepreneurial venture: When I was sixteen, I'd trek into Maryland with four of my buddies—several times a week, no less—to take a course in soccer refereeing. I was hooked early. I studied hard, learned all the rules (or, as they call them in soccer, "laws"), bought every book I could find—remember, this is well before Amazon—and attended every clinic I could get to. I would even talk my way into the "senior" clinics.

I was sixteen.

As it turns out, my friends and I were the first teenage referees in Northern Virginia—and among the first in the nation.

I took refereeing seriously—and I got good at it. Really good. So good that I never had to have a "real" job, all of the way through college. I made a ton of money refereeing soccer games.

I subscribed to a magazine called *Soccer America,* which was delivered to my home every single week, and I'd read it the moment it arrived. Once they even did a big article on me! There were a few ads in that magazine where you could mail order "soccer stuff:" Uniforms. Balls. Posters. You know the stuff.

So even though the sport was growing in popularity, spreading like wildfire in our community, most of the soccer stores were located mostly in New York and Pennsylvania. *Nothing in Virginia.* There was no place for anyone who wanted to buy soccer-related items to go locally.

I smelled opportunity.

I guess it was at that point that my entrepreneurial spirit really awakened. Low supply and high demand? Even my sixteen-year-old mind told me that this was the perfect combination. I didn't know how I'd do it *so I just started.*

I'd order products from the places I saw advertising in the soccer magazine—shorts, shin guards, screw-in studs, soccer-related trinkets—nothing that extravagant or expensive because I didn't have much money, but I just started.

Didn't ask anyone's permission.

Didn't draw up a business plan.

Didn't look to see if there were any rules about running a small business.

Didn't beg or borrow money.

Just did it.

Pretty quickly, I developed the reputation of being the guy you could turn to for just about anything you needed for the game. I had a small warehouse in my bedroom.

Guys started coming to me for all of their soccer needs—cleats, balls, shirts, you name it—and I'd even store some of my "inventory" in my school locker to sell to my high school teammates. I had a little black book—my very first ledger!—to help me keep track of all the orders. I never made a ton of money but I started to learn about business. I discovered that I had a knack for seeing opportunity. Lots of people had the same opportunity but no one else even tried.

A little philosophical side note: *There is no lack of opportunity in America. None. There is only a lack of ambition. Having worked with lawyers in all sizes of cities and towns, and in all consumer-oriented practice areas, I can tell you that the only difference between the super successful and happy lawyer and the rest is that the successful lawyer has a burning desire to get better, will search for models and resources and will execute on* *proven plans. For the most part, I can spend fifteen minutes with a lawyer, ask them a few questions, and predict their future.*

Looking back on it, I remember how confident all of this made me feel; how cool it felt to be the only person around who could actually satisfy such uniquely specialized requests. I'm sure this is where I get my self-confidence today. This is where it started.

It got to the point where I'd see a buddy walking down the hall or maybe on his way to soccer practice and I'd look down at his shoes and say, "Hey! What's with the shoes? Looks like you could really use a pair of Adidas cleats! I could get them for you in a size ten, and I can have them for you in less than a week!"

Profit wasn't my main concern back then (but it was cool to end up with more money than when I started). Looking back, my reputation as an entrepreneur began in the halls of Thomas Jefferson High School in Alexandria, Virginia.

Even though I didn't call it this back then, I was manifesting the very concepts and principles that I teach lawyers today in Great Legal Marketing:

1. Found something I liked doing;

2. That I was good at;

3. That the world needed; and

4. That the world would pay for. Bingo!

A Mentor and a Marketer: The Perfect Combination

Here's the story of how I became a leader in the "coaching to lawyers" world.

I got out of law school in 1983 and was hired by a small personal injury and medical malpractice defense firm. I was fortunate in that I got to try a lot of cases, including complex medical mal-practice cases in Virginia and the District of Columbia, in my first couple of years out of law school.

As that firm transitioned to a plaintiff's practice, I started trying and winning car accident and medical malpractice cases. At the same time, my family was growing and in 1995 I found myself coaching three soccer teams at once while trying to commute for-ty-five minutes each way to and from work.

Life was becoming complicated and I thought to myself, *I'm a pretty good lawyer and I'm getting good results, how hard could it be to start and run a law firm of my own, closer to home?*

So I left to start my next entrepreneurial venture. Just me and one assistant (my sister, Terry Patterson), setting up first in the spare office of a buddy of mine; then, shortly thereafter, leasing 1,100 square feet of space on Old Lee Highway right in the center of the City of Fairfax. (More on this later in the book.)

Because I had taken cases with me when I left my old firm, the new firm started well, but it wasn't long before I realized that I really knew nothing about the *business* of the practice of law: how to stand out amongst the personal injury crowd and attract clients; how to build a referral base; how to manage money; how to hire and fire employees.

One day I got a sales letter from Nightingale-Conant. I'd become a great fan (and follower) of success literature and had pur-chased a trunkful of tapes and books about selling, goal setting, and running a small business.

This sales letter was different. It was for a $300 product created by a man named Dan Kennedy and it was called "Magnetic Market-ing®." The advertisement promised that if I *invested in* the product I would soon have a steady stream of clients waiting for me outside my door. (More on this later, too.)

I bit on it even though at that time I didn't own any book, tape set, or instruction manual that had cost me more than $49.95, the standard price at that time for six audiocassettes.

Glad I did.

About a week later, the UPS guy brought me a box filled with audio tapes and a huge, three-ring binder. I took one look at the package and immediately started feeling buyer's remorse. How was I going to explain spending $300 for a three-ring binder to my wife, the bookkeeper? I decided I was going to return it as soon as I could, exercising the "no-questions-asked, money-back guarantee." It looked, after all, like a bunch of photocopied pages hole-punched and stuffed into the binder. As I thumbed through the binder I saw material for chiropractors, real estate agents, and plumbers. *None of this could possibly apply to lawyer,* I thought.

I do think that God spoke to me at that point and said, "Just listen to the tapes. No harm in that." So I stuffed them in my car and started listening to them as I drove to and from the office and to and from soccer games and practices.

They were fascinating. Dan Kennedy talked about a restaurant owner who did a "three-step mailing" to get customers and a plumber who used an "educational video" to sell more of his services. He talked about becoming an "invited guest" instead of an "annoying pest" with your advertising. I remember driving around in my car, listening to those cassette tapes, not fully understanding most of what I was listening to because it was such a different way of thinking; so revolutionary. I had never heard anything like this written or spoken about in the legal profession. But, after playing and rewinding, playing and rewinding those tapes time and time again, the material began to make sense!

My brain was on fire. I remember thinking to myself, *If I can just figure this stuff out . . . if I can just figure out a way to use these ideas in my law practice, then my life will change forever.*

My life did change. There are certain moments in your life where someone you meet, or some book you read, changes the *trajectory* of your life. I call them "God moments." This was one of them.

I started implementing the ideas of "information-based" marketing in my law practice. Lesson number one from Dan Kennedy: *stop doing what everyone else in your business is doing unless you want to remain average.*

What were all of the personal injury lawyers saying to the market at that time? "Injured? No Fee if No Recovery. Free Consultation. Call Now. We'll Get You All the Money You Deserve." (Come to think of it, these are the same messages used today. If you are a personal injury attorney you should be paying real close attention to this book now!)

Dan's message was that I could continue to try to compete in that big pond of messaging or I could start to think seriously about a different way of presenting myself to the market. I had tried option one and it wasn't getting me anywhere!

Nothing to lose by trying, I thought.

I started writing consumer white papers about, "What to do after you are injured in a car accident," and, "Why most medical malpractice claimants never recover a dime," and, "The secrets to getting your long-term disability benefits paid."

I was changing the way I marketed Ben Glass Law by giving consumers a reason to raise their hands, request our information, and start a conversation *before* they made a decision about hiring a lawyer. I was following up with this now much larger flow of prospects using CRM software called Infusionsoft. Education-based marketing plus interesting long-tail follow up brought in more of the larger injury and malpractice cases that I wanted to do. Importantly, it also repelled the cases that I no longer wanted.

(Remember, choose the life and practice *you* want and never feel guilty about saying no.)

Part of what I did as I was exploring the principles of Magnetic Marketing® was to look around to see if anyone else had "translated" the principles for the lawyer market. A few non-lawyers had tried, but those materials were not good. Not being lawyers, they didn't know that some of what they suggested violated lawyer marketing ethics and could actually get lawyers disbarred.

Note: *This is still a problem today. As a lawyer, you are responsible to your state bar with your marketing. Some of the non-lawyer gurus selling you, "The new way to build your practice" are actually dangerous to your license. They have no knowledge of, and little interest in, the ethics of lawyer marketing and if your ticket gets yanked they simply move on to their next victim.*

One of Dan's followers, *lawyer* Bill Hammond, in Overland Park, Kansas, had successfully used many of Dan's ideas to build a highly successful "Alzheimer's Law" practice. Bill very generously shared his materials and ideas with me early on to help me build a more solid practice based on Dan's Magnetic Marketing® principles.

Thank you, Bill.

The discovery and implementation of Magnetic Marketing® into my law practice changed the trajectory of my life. I immediately bought everything that I could find that Dan Kennedy had written. I found magicians, carpet cleaners, real estate agents, and chiropractors who were successfully using Dan's materials to improve their businesses. While most lawyers would have rejected examples from outside the legal industry ("we are *different*"), I embraced them. That sounded cool to me.

And my practice grew.

I teamed up with my friend Tom Foster (Foster Web Marketing) to create a kick-ass website that incorporated the "information-first + extensive follow-up" marketing and it was off to the races we went.

Through Dan Kennedy I met Bill Glazer (Dan later sold his company, Kennedy Inner Circle, to Bill, where it was renamed Glazer-Kennedy Inner Circle) and it was Dan and Bill who encouraged me to take what I had done in my practice and teach it to the lawyer market. Thus, Great Legal Marketing was born in an upstairs bedroom of my house.

Like my earlier decision to deal soccer equipment out of my office, I just started. No real business plan. Didn't wait for an invitation from my industry. I just got an idea, encouragement, and a new website that Tom Foster built for me and launched.

Thank you again, Dan, Bill, and Tom.

With the birth of Great Legal Marketing, I was able to bring the principles of Dan's Magnetic Marketing® to the tens of thousands of lawyers out there who, sure, might have been *great* lawyers (because law school and the professional "continuing legal education" courses, after all, teach you how to be a good lawyer), but didn't have a clue about how to market and sell themselves in our very crowded and competitive market. Without knowing how to market and sell legal services, it really doesn't matter how good of a lawyer you are. As I pointed out in the introduction, the profession continues to fail lawyers in this regard.

I unveiled GLM's philosophy to the lawyer market with my main message: *Being a good lawyer and being a good business person are two entirely different things. They require two entirely different skill sets. You will have a happier, more fulfilled journey through the profession if you are good at both and being good at both is good for clients.*

I knew there were tens of thousands of lawyers out there (still are) who don't have a clue about how to build a real *business* (and actively shun even thinking of their law firm as a business). Many want, but have no idea of how to navigate the balancing act of being a good lawyer, a good business person, and a family and community leader, as I have done.

Let me be clear: living life as a lawyer is not *easy* but it's *all* a lot harder if you don't think that being highly successful in the many realms of your life is possible and don't have an instruction manual to follow.

The skill sets that make a great lawyer are completely different—separate and district entities altogether—from the skills sets that make a great business leader. Accept this, and commit to working on the "business" part and you will change your life.

It took me a long time to 1) learn and 2) accept that truth.

And it was a truth that changed my life.

. . .

Today, I call Dan Kennedy one of my good friends.

Great Legal Marketing started by providing "marketing information to personal injury lawyers." It wasn't long before we attracted lawyers from across consumer law niches, and today our membership includes lawyers who practice family law, criminal/DUI defense, bankruptcy, estate planning, workers compensation, and the like. Yes, we even have "B2B" firms who have adopted our strategies to build practices that serve the lives these lawyers have chosen to live.

So as GLM grew into a national phenomenon, I made it a point to be as clear and concise in our mission as humanly possible. Though you'll see it again in successive chapters, I still want to offer up a concise summary of what we are and what we do.

Our mission: To teach lawyers how to build more profitable law practices that serve themselves, their families, their clients, and the community, *in that order.*

We shun the status quo. We put marketing at the top of our "skills to be learned" list because without good marketing it simply doesn't matter how good of a lawyer you are, or, frankly, how good your other business systems are.

No calls, no cases. Simple as that.

Our message: Decide on the kind of life *you* want to live, on the way *you* want to relate to the world and the people within it, then go about the business of making that life a reality. Build *your* business on it. And from that, everything else will flow. Oh, and ignore the critics you will hear from along the way. Have you noticed how those who remain mired in misery want you to join their drama?

Resist.

Our audience: My books, workshops, training sessions, and attention are geared to you, the solo and small firm attorney. You are heroic. You serve the community and your families better than the elites, often working without a huge safety net. Your state bar ignores you, not so much out of malice, but because it doesn't really know you.

I do.

I *am* you.

. . .

An Enduring Marketing Lesson from Dad!

Show up like nobody else. Yet again, a lesson that my father taught me very early on in life—and again, a lesson that I learned on the soccer field. And here, let me share a pivotal and powerful memory.

On the drive out to Sleepy Hollow Elementary School on the day in the spring of 1970 that I was going to try out for the Select Soccer team with the Annandale Boys Club—I was twelve years old—my father offered some sage advice.

Dad: When the coach asks, tell him you play left fullback.

Me: Okay, but can I ask you a few questions?

Dad: Sure, ask away.

Me: You know I'm right-footed, right? I can't kick a ball very far with my left foot.

Dad: Yes, I know that. I'm your father. I've been watching you play for three years.

Me: You know I've never played fullback, right?

Dad: Yup, you like to score goals and you are good at it.

Me: So, now tell me why I should tell the coach I play left fullback?

What my father said to me after that is something I will never forget:

> *"I know the other players who are trying out. They are all pretty good. They all like to score goals. They are all right-footed. No one else is going to tell the coach that they want to play left fullback, so if you speak up and say you do, you'll at least make it onto the team."*

I remember something clicking in my mind as he spoke, like the pieces of a jigsaw puzzle coming together. His words made sense. It was the wisest strategy of all: To show up like nobody else. Distinguish yourself by being different. Refuse to be a cookie-cutter.

Still, though, I expressed a little doubt. *Worry* was more like it. I knew nothing about playing fullback.

As usual, Dad seemed to read my mind.

"Don't worry yourself about it," he reassured me. "Worrying doesn't do any good anyway—in fact, it might just undercut your performance out there on the field. Just tell the coach you play left fullback. We'll figure the rest out later. *Just get onto the team!*"

So a few minutes later, we stood out on the field, and the coach, Dave Dugan, an Irish immigrant whose son, Doug, became one of my best friends, went around the team asking each of us what position we played. Everyone else wanted to play forward, of course—they wanted to score goals and run fast and preen their feathers in front of the cheering crowd—but when it came my turn, I answered him loud and clear:

"I play left fullback!"

And just as my wise father had predicted, Coach Dugan looked at me and said, "You're on the team."

So the lesson in this story is: Find a way to distinguish yourself from the crowd. Create a way to stand out. Look around, study what your competitors are doing, then figure out how you can do it differently. There is no "ladder of success" that you are required to climb for anything.

This is why I love my dad so much.

Because we were always figuring stuff out together.

By the way, six years later that team was national youth champions. Every player went on to play soccer in college and several, including Gary Etherington, Kip Germain, Chris Davin, Doug Dugan, and Carl Strong, went on to play professional soccer. I got a scholarship and played left fullback for William & Mary.

Thanks again, Dad.

. . .

The Responsibility Factor

I'm pretty sure that one of the main reasons I've been so successful in my business and my law practice is because I've always held myself to a ridiculously high standard. Being the best is the only option.

This means, of course, that when I get involved in a project or immerse myself in the process of learning about some new concept or idea that interests me, I tend to give 150 percent of my emotional and mental energy to the task; my default is to learn every single nook and cranny of whatever it is I'm studying. Again, this thirst to learn is in my DNA, and I'm absolutely certain that my parents put it there.

This kind of relentlessly thorough approach to learning (some would call it obsessive) also had a profound effect on my next entrepreneurial endeavor as a youth: becoming a soccer referee.

I mentioned that I studied hard about how to be the best referee I could be. I'd also mentioned that my buddies and I traveled to Maryland several times a week just to attend a clinic on refereeing.

Well, eventually, my buddies lost interest. They stopped attending the clinics and moved on to other things, developed other interests, as teenagers often do. Some quit because of the abuse that rains down on sports officials no matter what their age. But me? I stuck with it, enjoyed it immensely, and as a result, I really did get good. It was just a matter of a few years before I was "in the middle" of adult games and being selected to referee in tournaments and leagues around the region.

For me, refereeing was an early entrepreneurial endeavor. It taught me the value of leadership, patience, decision-making, showing up on time, and how to manage people—and I got paid for it! (If you have a teenager who is interested in soccer refereeing, reach out to me and I'll send you a free gift to inspire them!)

If that's not a business model for today's entrepreneur, then I don't know what is: find what you love to do, learn all about it, and run at it hard.

I guess the other factor, the other trait, that's vitally important if you want to succeed as a referee is establishing what I call a *responsibility factor*. The men and women who assigned referees to the games all knew me, respected me, and, yes, they even *liked* me, because I was punctual, knowledgeable, and dependable—even though I was just a teenager. I did what I said I would do. They never had to worry about me not showing up, on time, ready to go.

From refereeing what I learned was this: If you know the laws of the game backwards and forwards, if you show up on time to every single game—in the correct uniform and ready to get down to business—and if you're respectful of the players and can consistently demonstrate a high level of confidence and excellence, then you will be noticed, and will often get the plumb assignments together with the respect of coaches, assigners, players, and the other referees. The formula for success is rarely hidden inside some black box.

At the risk of sounding immodest, I need to say it again: I was good at what I did. Articles about me showed up in soccer books and magazines. Looking back at what I accomplished, I'd learned to become great at *my* game—the game of soccer—and great at *the* game—the game of life.

Make no mistake about it, refereeing was not easy for me.

Many of the youth coaches in the '70s were foreign-born and they often thought they knew everything about soccer—*certainly* more than this skinny American teenager. Many times I walked off of a field having been the object of intense verbal abuse.

Awful stuff.

There were many times I guess I could have quit, but that thought never actually crossed my mind. My commitment was to continue to know more about the game than they did. This was a lot harder, pre-Internet, but every time I saw a book that had anything to do with sports officiating, I bought it. Anytime there was a high-end clinic, I attended it. Anytime I had the opportunity to work with a more experienced referee, I took it. My learning continues and today in my home library I have one of the largest collection of soccer referee biographies and autobiographies in the world. (Here's a thought if you have a kid interested in refereeing: get them a few of those biographies. Know what you will find inside? Failure. Bad days. Times they wanted to quit. Good stuff for young minds who want to be successful in the face of adversity.)

My reputation grew and grew, to the point where the assigners would automatically assign me to some of the best games.

What was nice was that they knew they didn't have to worry about anything when I was out there on the field—and it was their confidence in me that helped bolster my own confidence, in myself.

Plus, at the end of the season, I'd get a check for $300 or $350, which, to me, was like somebody handing me a bag of gold!

The funny thing was that, because I loved doing it so much, it never really felt like *work*. By that I mean it didn't feel like a laborious task—not like selling furniture or flipping burgers or pumping gas.

No, this was something else: This was actually *fun*. Kind of like my law firm today.

(There are many great youth referees today. The problem is that most don't last more than two years. If you Google "Ben Glass Soccer Sportsmanship Challenge" you will see some of the work I am doing in that area to improve those statistics today. And, in case you are wondering, yes, I'm still able to keep up with sixteen-to eighteen-year-olds and still referee high school soccer and youth travel games!)

Note: *Richard Broad, long-time friend and former college soccer coach, recently asked me why I never pursued refereeing on a professional level. My answer was quite simple: at the time when I could have made a decision to "keep climbing the*

referee ladder," my family was growing. I had always thought
that blending a professional refereeing career with the autonomy
of working in (or running) a small law firm was very doable.
What I discovered was that the travelling required with pro-
fessional refereeing was, for me, incompatible with raising a
family. I simply prioritized family over refereeing.

Wisdom with Staying Power

So here are a few other marketing principles—a few other life
lessons—that you can easily carry over into the present day, and
that can help you meet (and exceed) your goal of building a better
life for yourself. I consider myself fortunate and blessed to have
learned so many of these lessons early in life, during my early entrepreneurial days:

Be a forever learner. No matter how much you think you
know about your business, you can always learn more. Each year
I *read* forty to fifty business books, not including the audio books
I *listen* to while commuting. This is one of the values to which we
ascribe in both my law firm and my marketing company—that
each lawyer in my firm and every member of GLM becomes (and
remains) what we call a "forever learner."

Build your business from a place of confidence. I've already
described the heightened feeling of self-confidence I experienced
during my first few entrepreneurial encounters. Nurturing this
self-confidence at all times is vital; it sends the signal to your
clients, your customers, and your competition that you will not
be bullied, threatened, or encroached upon. Figuring out why you
deserve a place in the market, first, will serve you well here. I once
heard a lawyer say that he couldn't figure out anything that distinguished him from every other injury lawyer out there. I felt sorry

for him. He should have looked for another profession. A great way to nurture your self-confidence is to . . .

Hang out with people who are better than you are. Here again, my father's wisdom became my own: That very team that I placed onto? The team that now had a new left fullback?

Our 1976 youth national championship was achieved because we always played up. We always played teams that were older, stronger, and faster than we were. Sometimes we got our butts kicked. In high school we combined college visits with scrimmages against the college varsity teams.

I can clearly remember, just a few weeks before our June 1976 national championship game in New York against our familiar foes, Chicago Sparta (another team filled with the next generation of college and professional players), getting taken apart by a travelling German youth team on our home field! This is the best way to *get good*.

One of our GLM members, a now very successful attorney, flunked out of college on his first try. After they let him back in a year later the first thing he did was form a study group that you could only be a part of if you had a B+ average or higher. No one ever asked him what his average was, since he started the group. He ended up graduating with honors. He played up!

In athletics and in business, the path to success is to surround yourself with people who are better than you. Always try to "play up" by surrounding yourself with people (not just lawyers but people from all walks of life) who are smarter and more accomplished than you are. It pushes you beyond your limits.

In fact, it creates *new limits* which you never even thought you'd be able to surpass . . . and probably wouldn't have surpassed had you not deliberately placed yourself in the position to grow. (More on this later in the book.)

Again, it was the game of soccer, playing and refereeing, that really helped solidify some of the most important values that I'd ever learn in the business world, the legal world, and in the daily world of life and living. Soccer spurred my entrepreneurial spirit.

Soccer, and of course, my dad.

. . .

But let's get back to my high school locker.

The Made-up Mandate

The business-out-of-my locker experience that I described earlier was only the tip of my entrepreneurial iceberg. Sure, I might have only been sixteen, but when other "business opportunities" presented themselves, I was ready to take full advantage of them.

Take the Case of the Red Shorts.

Keep in mind that all of this was happening in the '70s, when everybody desperately wanted to be *cool*. Well, the athletic director of our school definitely wasn't what you'd call a soccer guy—football and baseball were more his speed—and he wasn't the least bit interested in a proper soccer uniform.

So, when he *did* order soccer stuff for us, he'd order it either from a football or a general sports catalog.

Well, wearing a football jersey and pretending it was a soccer jersey was simply not cool *at all*, so my buddy and I decided we simply weren't having it.

So what did we do? One day before the spring soccer season began, the two of us—his name was Fraser Burns—took a little trip to Sears to have a look around.

We found some red men's shorts that looked *just like* soccer shorts. Well, at least they looked more like soccer shorts than the general P.E. shorts the athletic director was making us wear . . . so we bought all of them!

Fortunately for us, Sears prided itself on keeping a healthy inventory of red shorts, because we were actually able to find about twenty pairs that very day! (Thank you, Sears, and sorry you eventually got the business part completely wrong and folded.)

Fraser and I took all those red shorts home and cut the tags out of them so none of our teammates would know they came from Sears, or how much they cost. Then we put new price tags on them and the next day, we told the entire team that they *had* to wear those red shorts at our games. (We were the captains; they did what we told them to do.)

"It's been decided that we *have* to wear these red shorts—all of us," we said with authority. "So here are yours, and here are yours, and it's gonna be five dollars. Pay Fraser as you leave the locker room!"

It was a fake mandate, of course—nobody but Fraser and I had said *anything* about the team being required to wear red shorts to the game—but I guess because we sounded so convincing, it actually *worked*.

It worked!

And we sold every pair.

I suppose the lesson in all of that is to believe in yourself so fiercely that other people believe in you, too.

Even if it means issuing a made-up mandate.

Fill in the Blanks

Particularly in the world of refereeing, what I learned was this:

If you know and understand the laws of the game backwards and forwards, if you do what you say you'll do (show up on time to every single game, with the right mindset), if you lead the players and consistently demonstrate a high level of confidence and excellence, then you will become great at the craft.

Because every word of the paragraph you just read can so easily be applied to today's solo and small firm lawyer, I'll just write the paragraph over, filling in a few different words. This fill-in-the-blank exercise is positive proof that the concepts of Great Legal Marketing have genuine staying power.

For you, small firm attorney, the hero of family and icon to your community, what I learned was this:

> *If you know and understand how today's consumers make deci-sions about solving their legal issues, do what you say you'll do (don't over-promise and underperform). With the right mindset, if you lead your employees and can consistently demonstrate a high level of confidence and excellence, then you will be great at the craft of being a law firm leader.*

> *And hero.*

> *And icon.*

I'd ask you, here, to return to the italicized paragraphs above.

Go back and reread them yet again. See how closely they align. What this means, of course, is that every principle and concept I've shared from my own life can be applied—directly and consistent-ly—to your life in the legal and/or business world.

I guarantee that the "lawyer wellness" issue would vastly improve if more in the profession would stop thinking like lawyers and begin looking at how other successful people have engineered their businesses to attain a happier life.

Full Circle, All Over Again

It wasn't until I started writing this book, really—not until I had a reason and a rationale for reflecting back on my days as a kid, a teenager, and a young renegade attorney—that I've come to fully realize how much overlap there is in my life.

I feel blessed that so much of what I've learned in the past is precisely what I'm teaching lawyers today. What this tells me is that principles and practices like this live—and last—forever. They endure. They stand up to the test of time.

It's no coincidence, then, that even though my father worked a demanding, full-time job as an electrical engineer, he also made it a priority to spend time with his wife and seven children.

Today, I do the same thing. Sure, running both a marketing consulting business and a law firm takes time and energy, but by practicing the well-proven principles of Magnetic Marketing® as "translated" by me for our world, I've been able to both run a successful practice and *still get home in time for dinner.* More importantly, thousands of lawyers are now following in my footsteps.

Now it's time to make these principles and philosophies apply to your own practice. Start here:

1. Decide what you want your life to be.

2. Decide the type of practice that is aligned with that life.

3. Decide what type of client supports that practice.

The rest of the "formula" is:

4. Figuring out the marketing that will attract that client.

5. Getting those clients to "multiply" by referral.

6. Building a team and systems that makes the experience of working with you and your firm memorable.

There's no other way to say it: Decide what your dreams will be, decide what makes you happy, then do everything in your power to build your business—and your life—around that.

The minute you become an active member of Great Legal Marketing, you, too, can join me on this journey. Attract more (and better) clients. Improve your quality of life. Create a happier home, all by ascribing to principles you'll find within GLM.

The best time to figure out how to run a profitable practice that's also fun and good for the family was *before you started the practice*.

The next best time is now.

CHAPTER THREE
THE TWELVE-YEAR TRAJECTORY
LAW SCHOOL, FIRST JOB, AND THE FIRST OF MANY FIRSTS

Early Decision

I was sixteen when I knew I wanted to become a lawyer.

I knew I enjoyed figuring things out and solving complex problems. I also knew I was good at it. I was a tinkerer and a problem-solver, a lot like my father, only Dad came at it from his perspective as an electrical engineer. I had a first grade teacher who told me I was lazy. I wasn't. I was just trying to get beyond her "make-work" and onto something more interesting. As early as first grade, I rebelled against doing the same thing that everyone else was doing "just because that's the way we've always done it."

I consider myself blessed to have made the decision to pursue law as a career so early in life because it meant that from that point forward, everything I did was directed towards this goal.

I almost wish I could say that I was this super-insightful sixteen year old who'd crafted this carefully-conceived life plan, but that just wasn't the case. In fact, I didn't come to the decision completely on my own at all.

It came *to me.*

In high school.

I had an English teacher who'd let me read anything I wanted to read. I found myself drawn to books by or about lawyers, like F. Lee Bailey's *For the Defense* and *Helter-Skelter* by Vincent Buglosi and Curt Gentry. I liked watching TV shows about law, too. This stuff was fascinating to me, and I consumed anything I could get my hands on about not just the practice of the law, but about the people who practiced it.

Lawyers like F. Lee Bailey were inspiring to me. He was obviously very good at his craft, but the fact that he *knew* he was good made him even better. He never appeared to question himself. Never seemed to struggle with low self-confidence or *negative internal self-talk.*

I didn't have a lot of negative self-talk, either. I was too naïve to know just how much hard work my journey would entail.

A sidebar message here on the dangers of self-doubt:

> *Your thoughts do become your reality. While self-doubt is a normal part of the human experience, never succumb to negative thinking, especially the negative talk of others. Rid your life of "negative Nellies." An occasional crisis of confidence is normal, especially if you're doing something new, but don't let it control your life.*

Be bold in your self-confidence. For young lawyers, here are some tips about your early trials:

1. *Everyone in the courtroom is afraid. Gerry Spence taught me that. (If you don't know who Gerry Spence is, find a copy of* Gunning for Justice *and read it.)*

2. *Walk into the courtroom like you own it (and everybody in it).*

3. *Make sure the jury sees you as the voice of authority—even above the judge. Be the leader.*

4. *Don't worry about every little thing that could go wrong in the trial. Your mind is powerful. It will find everything that could go wrong if you give it permission to. The vast majority of the things we worry about don't even come close to actually occurring.* Worry does you no good. In fact, it does you significant harm.

5. *Remember that nobody in the world could try your case against you as well as you could try your case against you. Period. (If in doubt, re-read #4.)*

. . .

I've always been very clear about *why* I wanted to become a lawyer. In fact, the reason I wanted to go into law is as simple and straightforward as my reason for *not* wanting to.

I never went into law for the sole reason of helping others or because I wanted to devote myself to a life of service, suffering, and sacrifice. Instead, I found the work interesting and thought I'd be good enough at it to make money.

The practice of law is an opportunity for you to maximize your gifts for the benefit of your family and the client in a win-win deal. It's a *business*. I never accepted the notion that a life of law meant a lifetime of altruistic sacrifice and noble suffering. That wasn't my vision of a productive life worth living.

I Went Into Law Because I Knew I Would Be Good at It

So at sixteen, I was already very clear on what I wanted and even clearer on the steps I needed to take to get there. It was this awareness, combined with the decision to work as hard I possibly could to become the best that I could possibly be, that gave me the momentum I needed to make it happen. Period.

That, and the fact that I didn't have any naysayers in my life telling me I wasn't right about my future. (I did have a high school guidance counselor who, when she saw the very few schools that I had applied to, told me that I wasn't smart enough to get into William & Mary, let alone think about becoming a lawyer. I told her I already had a soccer scholarship there, so she might as well update her records.)

I didn't know it at the time, but even as a teenager I was iden-tifying (and living out) the central principles of Great Legal Mar-keting, namely:

- Figuring out what made me happy (you live for your life)

- Deciding what I needed to do get there (it's your respon-sibility)

- Building my life around this goal (doing things purpose-fully)

It was a great plan then, for a young man of sixteen years old trying to figure out his place in the world.

And it's a great plan now, for lawyers who are trying to figure out how to realign their priorities, strengthen their practice, and live exactly the kind of lives they want to live. The solo and small firm market gives you enormous flexibility for "life design."

It all boils down to this: The principles of GLM stand the test of time.

Learning to Learn

I attended the George Mason University School of Law (now the Antonin Scalia Law School) in Arlington, Virginia. By the time I graduated in 1983, I'd come to realize that *how* I learned was every bit as important as *what* I learned. This was, for me, a life-changing distinction.

In high school, I was a pretty solid student. I kept pace with the level of learning that was required of me at the time. In college, it took me about two years to learn how to study at a college level. (I was, after all, playing soccer and dating my future wife!) In law school, it took me about a year to figure out how to study effectively at the law school level.

Being aware of these *patterns of learning*, to me, was just as important as learning the material itself. Even as a teenager, I was always keenly aware of exactly what I needed to do to get ahead of the curve, to stay ahead of that curve, and to ultimately reach (and exceed) my goal—and the answer, of course, was to study, study, study. Plan, plan, plan. In retrospect, being painfully shy helped too. I didn't have much of a social life in high school.

I've already explained that this was exactly how I became one of the best youth soccer referees in Northern Virginia in the '70s (and probably the country)—through hard work, preparation, and constant studying.

When it comes to learning a new subject or taking on a new project, this is my mantra:

Know your subject better than anybody else and do whatever it takes to become the best at it. No matter how complicated the task or difficult the subject, it can be mastered. **Anything can be learned.**

The same principle held true in law school.

I went into law school with the attitude that any and everything can be mastered through study, no matter how difficult or challenging.

Here's a good example of how that mindset made a difference during law school: I got straight A's in my tax law classes. As any lawyer knows, tax law is complex and arcane. I sucked at math but I understood the tax code. Most of my law school classmates dreaded tax class, even though they had voluntarily signed up for it; they considered it ridiculously complicated and difficult to grasp.

Their downfall, of course, was that they went into it with the wrong mindset. They believed they would suck at it and then set out to prove that to themselves. As I said before, the mind is a powerful thing. It can accomplish just about anything you tell it to accomplish, including *failure*.

Failure, for me, was never an option. Neither was mediocrity.

I was also a voracious reader (still am). I'd devour any legal magazine or law journal I could get my hands on (still do). It didn't matter whether it was a book or an audio tape or a newsletter. If it was related to the practice or the principles of law, I snapped it up. As a young lawyer I was surprised to see law journals and magazines come into the office and pile up, unread.

Not just in law school but in life, I came to understand that there was a direct correlation between purposeful working and achievement. For me, the two things went hand in hand.

As my friend Dan Kennedy says, "It's really no mystery why some people are highly successful. The mystery is why more people are not highly successful."

This desire to want *to learn to learn* and to work hard at it, no matter where we are in life, is what defines us as forever learners, a concept I touched on in the previous chapter. The process of learning (not just about law but about life) is ongoing; it never stops.

For me, being a forever learner is not just a goal but a value. We don't hire people that we are not convinced "buy into" this philosophy.

The Power of the Mastermind

I devote an entire chapter to this subject later in the book, but I want to introduce it here because it's an important lesson that greatly influenced the course of the twelve-year trajectory I describe in this chapter: *Always surround yourself with people who are farther along the journey of success than you. Let them lift you up to a level of excellence you couldn't possibly achieve by yourself.*

Sound familiar? It should.

It's the same concept I practiced years earlier out on the soccer field. *Playing up* was the way our team got good enough to be national champions. The concept worked, so I carried it over with me into law school. Only this time, I wasn't standing on a soccer field.

I was sitting in a study group.

It might sound fairly benign, but inserting myself into a study group of the smart students was one of the smartest things I did in law school. Looking back, it was my first mastermind group, even though I had no idea what a "mastermind" group was back then.

The idea, of course, was that you were much more likely to make it through the "game of law school"—and increase your overall competitive advantage—by *tapping the brains of* a small groups of classmates who were smarter than you, instead of going it alone. Since I wasn't that smart, I was able to leverage the expertise of some of my smarter classmates.

Author and entrepreneur Jim Rohn famously said, "You are the average of the five people you hang out with most." If you aren't totally satisfied that you are getting all that you want out of your practice, then you need to reexamine and perhaps change your set of friends. Most lawyers are miserable. The idea is to not hang out with "most lawyers." I don't.

Lemons into Lemonade

I was fortunate to have had a couple of great mentors in law school, both of them law professors who influenced the overall trajectory of my life: Ray Benzinger and John Costello.

Fortunately for me, Benzinger, who taught contracts, and Costello, who taught Criminal Law and Ethics, were both real-life guys who'd been out in the world practicing law; winning and losing cases; writing briefs; taking depositions; and living lives that were full, balanced, and meaningful.

They were not theorists and they let it be known that they were not there to offer theoretical advice.

Looking back on it now, I'm sure they both recognized the unique challenges their students were facing—and they did everything in their power to help us push through.

At that time, the George Mason University School of Law was brand new. In fact, when I entered in the fall of 1980, it had just received its full American Bar Association (ABA) accreditation. Nobody paid it much attention and it was still struggling to find its footing. This didn't mean the school was fighting a *bad* reputation as much as it was trying to establish a good one. It had opened only one year earlier. (There was a predecessor school that was founded in 1972, but GMUSL was itself sanctioned in July 1979.)

Keep in mind, too, that the super-competitive Washington, D.C. region boasted some of the best law schools in the nation, among them Georgetown University, American University, George

Washington University, Catholic University, University of Virginia, and the University of Richmond.

What all of this meant, of course, was that nobody was knocking down our doors to recruit us; certainly not the major firms, anyway. Why *would* they, with some of the finest law schools in the country just a stone's throw away?

All of these factors—the newness of the law school, the ruthlessly competitive law school market in the D.C. area, and the fact that these two guys were more roll-up-your sleeves, real-life, we-don't-give-a-damn lawyers than prickly academicians—could have easily stacked the deck against me. There were a lot obstacles to overcome.

Instead, thanks in large part to Professors Benzinger and Costello, we turned lemons into lemonade.

Both Benzinger and Costello did everything within their power to teach us about the *practice* of law—real life stuff. Both of them devoted incredible amounts time and energy to helping students become *real lawyers* out there in a super competitive world.

They knew the obstacles we were about to face in the real world, even if we still didn't. They knew we weren't going to be regarded with a great deal of respect, or even recruited by anyone. At the time, I didn't really know any better. Didn't know you were *supposed* to go to a more prestigious law school. But I turned out okay. It's probably why I tell college students today to not waste their money going to the *best* law schools because where you go to school plays little part in what you will get out of the profession. It's a non-factor for 95 percent of law students.

Going to George Mason did play a major part in my life: it's how I met Bill Artz.

Twelve-Year Trajectory (1983–1995)

I've already briefly described how I landed a job as a law clerk for a very well-known Virginia attorney named Bill Artz while I was still in law school. I worked for Bill for about a year and a half before I graduated.

At about the same time I graduated, Bill was starting a new law firm with two of his buddies. Fortunately for me, they hired me as an associate. That was in 1983. I was making $15,000 a year.

And I was in heaven.

I had a good job as a practicing attorney, learning from a group of guys who were very, very good at their craft. I remember thinking to myself, *This is the greatest thing in the world! Somebody's paying me to solve problems and figure stuff out!*

There couldn't have been a better combination.

From the very beginning, they allowed me to become deeply involved in the actual *practice* of law, attending hearings, taking depositions, trying cases—the real-life work that's necessary for a lawyer to *get good*.

Here again, I was fortunate to be able to surround myself with lawyers who were better than I was. Smarter than I was. More experienced than I was. Playing up.

The cases we handled were complex and challenging, usually with lots of lawyers on each side. They trusted me enough to let me take the ball and run with it. Over time, I learned to trust myself at least enough to know that I was turning into a pretty darned good trial lawyer.

The Case of the Disappearing "Why"

As talented as these guys were, and as much as I learned from them during the time we practiced together, I was feeling more and more drawn to the *business* of lawyering.

I remember recommending a few new marketing ideas and a couple of different strategies that might have helped us boost the business—starting a new newsletter, maybe, or taking out a bold new ad in the Yellow Pages—but these "outside the box" ideas never really seemed to gain any traction.

So what I was left with was a group of excellent lawyers who didn't seem all that interested in figuring out the business side of the practice. They were satisfied with their level of knowledge in a way that I knew I never could be.

In today's world, this is the norm rather than exception: Most great lawyers are great at being lawyers but not so great at running a business. For those of us with entrepreneurial DNA, this is frustrating. We just see the world differently.

Looking back on it now, I'm sure that even that philosophical divide was a blessing; maybe a gentle nudge from God to move on, push out in some new directions.

These three lawyers—fine trial lawyers, all of them—had formed a partnership and entered into a five-year lease for office space, but within eighteen months they were divorced as a partnership, so none of us were going anywhere since we still had a lease. That was a ton of fun. I just kept my head down and worked.

Though they would eventually splinter off and go their separate (and very successful) ways, they'd taught me another important lesson—and this is one of the main principles we teach in Great Legal Marketing: *In a law firm, the owners need to figure out the firm's purpose, reason for being, overall mission up-front and early on, so that everyone will remain on the same page moving forward.* Most law firm partnerships fail miserably at this, having formed a firm because everyone thought it would be "fun" to work together.

From working with thousands of solo and small firms across the country, this is what we know:

*Most law firms don't place a high priority on philosoph-
ical alignment—in agreeing on why your firm exists, on
what kinds of cases you're going to take, on what kinds of
risks you're going to absorb—and it is this lack of cohesion
that leads to unhappiness, disappointment, and ultimately, failure.*

The sooner you can identify and articulate the common vision
of your firm to partners, employees and clients, the better. This not
only assures that everyone is moving in the same direction but it
will also provide the entire foundation for your overall marketing
strategy and business decisions.

Look, it's okay for a bunch of friends to get together to form a
"firm" with each "partner" being responsible for his share of overhead,
but essentially running a "firm within a firm." That's fine if done by
deliberate choice, but understand that you are not actually building
a business. A business takes on a life of its own and can provide for
you even when you are not there. We are building businesses because
lawyers who build real business are happier.

You Never Forget Your First "Firsts"

I've never met a lawyer who can't remember their first "first."

Their first trial. Their first hung jury. Hearing that first knock
on the door before the jury reads that first verdict in a career. It's
important to go back and remember your "firsts," just because they
were pivot points that helped set the course of your trajectory. (It's
important, as we will see, to create your next "first" as you begin to
change your life and your practice.)

My First Malpractice Trial

I was a young lawyer, probably four years out of law school, when I was assigned the case of Catherine Groom, a kind and grandmotherly woman, now long since deceased, who'd had hip surgery performed by one of the pioneers of hip replacement surgery in America, Charles Engh, Sr., M.D.

I was up against a very big insurance company and an excellent defense lawyer who were both fully confident they were going to kick my butt. In addition to being world-famous himself for his pioneering work in porous-coated implants (implants that did not require cement), Dr. Engh had a very well-qualified expert witness from the University of Virginia. The entire team was confident and ridiculously self-assured. I was scared out of my mind. (All that stuff I wrote about earlier about "worry" and "no one can try the case against you as well as you could"—I learned that later. This was my first major trial as a plaintiff's lawyer.)

Our claim was that Dr. Engh had committed medical malpractice by waiting too long to remove an infected hip prosthesis that he had recently implanted to replace a first generation cemented implant. When he attempted to remove it, her femur fractured, and she was left infected and permanently disabled.

I remember thinking how great it was that Ms. Groom and her family had placed their full trust in me to handle—and win—their case. And just as I approached everything, I worked and worked and worked. Prepared and prepared and prepared. It was my M.O., and the only way I knew how to deal with my sense of inadequacy.

The insurance company offered no money to settle the case. I'd studied every related case, memorized the relevant law, and knew the medical history of Ms. Groom backwards and forwards. Plus, I wasn't at all in the mood to get my butt kicked. I wanted to win.

So I won.

I went in and won it.

We tried the case in the federal court in Alexandria, Virginia. The jury awarded Ms. Groom a half a million dollars, which was a lot in the medical malpractice world in Virginia in 1987.

I'll never, ever forget that feeling—a mix of euphoria for me and of tremendous relief for Mrs. Groom. Every lawyer remembers that first big win. I remember standing in the courtroom, waiting for the decision to be read aloud after hearing the knock from the jury room, and hearing the words:

We the jury, on the issue joined between Catherine Groom, the plaintiff and Charles Engh, M.D., the defendant, find in favor of the plaintiff and award her $500,000.

Rock and roll. Good guys: 1. Evil Empire Insurance Company: 0.

Ms. Groom invited me out to her house in Southern Maryland after the trial for soft-shell crabs. She also presented me with my "trophy:" the actual hip implant Engh had originally removed. It sits on the windowsill at my office.

That's how we celebrated the verdict.

Years later, a member of the jury saw me in a store. She stopped me and told me the jury felt that I had really cared about my client while Dr. Engh and his team were arrogant. Some of the members of the jury had wanted to award $750,000, the state maximum at the time. That would have been cool.

My First Personal Injury Trial

This was my first trial ever representing the plaintiff by myself. My wife Sandi and my mom even came to watch—which increased the pressure even more.

I was representing a guy whose car had been hit by a cab driver; an intersection accident, with no witnesses. We weren't asking for a lot in damages but he did have some medical bills. The insurance company we were up against hadn't offered us a cent.

I was trying the case against a very seasoned defense attorney, my wife and mother were sitting in the courtroom to hear me try this case, and all I remember thinking was, *Oh my God. I'm wasting the time of these seven jurors because this case is so small and it doesn't really matter all that much, in the larger scheme of things.*

Again, this was my own self-doubt talking, of course. My own momentary lack of confidence. (All that "control the courtroom stuff?" That came later, too!)

We ended up trying the case for a day, and then the jury couldn't decide! They were hung!

So we settled the case—and my first personal injury case also became my first hung jury case.

It seems anti-climactic now, but it definitely didn't seem anti-climactic as it the scene was unfolding. I can still picture my young wife and mom sitting proudly in the courtroom.

Go back and try to remember your first case. Your first hung jury. Your first verdict. No matter how long ago it was, my guess is that you still remember just about every detail.

This twelve-year trajectory was far more than just the first twelve years of my legal life: these were the years that gave rise to the rest of my entire life, and every one of those encounters has led me to precisely this point in life where I am right now.

So "Your First" is actually much, more than your first.

It's the beginning of a trajectory that will define the rest of your entire life.

Every aspect of that life—your lawyering life, your personal life, your family life, the business paths you choose to take—all of it belongs to *you*. This becomes a part of your unique story—a story no one can take from you.

. . .

But my life was changing, too. My family was expanding. I was doing pretty well at trying—and winning—cases. My reputation was growing.

But I also felt like I was being pulled. I'd mentioned earlier that during this time, I found myself coaching three soccer teams at once and making the grueling forty-five-minute commute to and from work each and every day, all while beginning to handle a larger and more complex caseload.

Something larger was calling. I remember thinking to myself, *Okay, so I know I'm a good lawyer. I win cases. I've got a strong reputation. Why not try something different?*

Why not strike out on my own? How hard could that be?

It was a question I would soon answer.

CHAPTER FOUR
HOW HARD CAN THIS BE?
TO START A LAW FIRM, START A LAW FIRM.

Forty-Five Minutes

I started my own law firm because I knew I'd be good at it. (Sound familiar? It's basically the same reason I listed in the previous chapter about why I wanted to become a lawyer.)

Even more important was the fact the entrepreneurial spirit that had started in the halls of my high school and had blossomed as I cashed those referee checks was bursting at the edges. We were a team of good lawyers, but there was nothing entrepreneurial about my first firm. We were very much "status quo" and "inside the box" when it came to the business side of the practice of law. Status quo is, by definition, "average." I didn't want to be average.

I was eager to begin making things happen for myself.

I saw opportunity that could not be acted upon because, "We've never done it that way before." Like Marty and Alex, the zebra and lion in *Madagascar* who get bored with life inside the zoo and conspire with the penguins to escape to the wild, I was ready to get out. There had to be something better "on the other side."

Note: *If you have children, you likely know who I am referring to. If not, Google it*

But the most important reason of all for wanting to strike out on my own?

My family life was getting complex, and controlling that was a primary value.

During the times when I should have been out on the soccer field with my children—at one point, I was coaching three different teams at the same time—I was either sitting in a conference room with clients or sitting in traffic on Interstate 395, trying *to get to* a conference room to meet with clients.

The way it was working out, I was usually barely able to leave the office in time enough to make it to their practices, which usually started in the later afternoon. And when I did get there, I often felt frustrated. Agitated. Wound up. D.C.-area traffic will do that to you.

To some, this might sound like a featherweight reason to even add to the list of reasons for my wanting to start my own firm, but I'm going to add it anyway since it played a big factor and many lawyers just "give in" to it.

The commute was killing me. As I just mentioned, it was a minimum of forty-five minutes each way—and that's not even allowing for traffic, unexpected accidents, or detours along the way. Our offices were in Rosslyn, Virginia, which sits on the bank of the Potomac River just up the way from Ronald Reagan Washington National Airport. We were in a high-rise that was nice, but the location made little sense. All of the lawyers lived at least forty-five minutes away. Plus, it wasn't all that convenient to clients, either.

Forty-five minutes, in my mind anyway, might just as well have been four hours and, looking back, I can't imagine why any of us put up with it for so long.

Here's how I see it: *Any* length of time is insufferable if you're spending it knowing that you'd rather be somewhere else, doing something else—like watching your children grow up.

This was fixable, in my view. *Why should a good lawyer have to accept a long and unpredictable commute as a given?* I thought.

I liked coaching soccer. I liked practicing law. I did not like driving to and from the workplace, so I decided to make a big change in my life.

Here's the thing: For the most part, my life was good.

It just didn't belong to me.

Here's what I say to GLM lawyers all the time, and it's the concept that really pushed me to stop putting up with things that were not consistent with my goals and to start my own firm:

Life is not a dress rehearsal. You only get one chance to live it, so try to do it right. Try to make decisions that make sense to you.

Family first.

I still live that way.

So in a very real way, the span of forty-five minutes (repeatedly, that is) is what helped push me towards striking out on my own.

And since we're on the subject of happiness, let me make this simple point again:

Too many young lawyers today are living under the mistaken impression that a minimum sixty-hour workweek is the norm; that happiness should be set aside until you have "climbed the ladder of success;"

and that even after you have checked off the boxes the profession has laid out for you, happiness should not come from the self-satisfaction of having pursued and achieved a goal YOU set, but rather should be derived from the pats on the back you get from the elite for working all those hours and volunteering for all those bar committees.

This is ridiculous. What young lawyers are learning is that to be happy, you've got to be sad. You've got to suffer. You've got to work grueling hours, play by other people's rules, and face the fact that you won't always be there for your kids and spouse when they need you.

There is no reason to accept this nonsense anymore. None. Stop listening to them.

If You're Not Happy With Your Life, Change It

By the time I packed up my cases and left the firm that by then had become Shevlin & Glass, I'd obviously learned a lot about the law, built a good reputation, and had good cases. Even though my wife Sandi and I had, only six months before, signed on to a giant mortgage in order to build a brand new house on three acres in Fairfax County, she and I chose family relationships over everything else.

I knew beyond the shadow of a doubt that we would figure out the money/business part. I just didn't know how long it would take.

Many lawyers will recite the mantra of "family comes first," but their actions shout otherwise. If I follow you around for a week, what conclusion would I draw from what I observe about your behavior?

One more time:

Protecting and providing for your family is the most important goal you will ever have.

So yes, it's accurate to say that at this point in my life, I felt like I was being pulled in a lot of different directions. I was a good lawyer. Family was calling. Sandi and I were involved with our church and with the kids' school. I wanted to be there with my children, not just as their coach, but as their father and I was beginning to develop that entrepreneurial "itch."

After not too much longer, God began to put it in my heart that *I could make a living while making a life. I didn't know exactly how this was going to happen since I had no model to study at that point, but I was a good listener.*

. . .

As I've mentioned, my priorities weren't really all that out of whack.

I *knew* I wanted and needed to put my family first . . . I just didn't exactly how to do it.

I *knew* that I was a good lawyer who'd probably be able to start a new law firm that would not only succeed but thrive . . . I just wasn't entirely sure what steps I needed to take to get me there. I was feeling restless and ready to stretch out into new territory because, yes, life inside a zoo is boring.

I had been around enough older, miserable lawyers to know that the endgame many had seemingly accepted—broken families, long hours of stress every week, extreme financial ups and downs— didn't seem to be worth it. I also did not want to be like many of them were: experts at the "blame game."

At that point in my career I attended lots of lawyer conferences and volunteered for lots of committees. Hang out with lawyers and it's pretty easy to get sucked into whining: whining about judges, insurance companies, and other lawyers.

I need to veer off for a second here to examine the subject of the blame game because it is critical to your future.

Having now had the experience of hanging out with thousands of lawyers who are actually thrilled to be practicing law, I can tell you that the most successful believe in these principles:

- Never blame anyone else for the mistakes you've made in your own life.

- Where you are today is a direct result of the decisions that you've made in the past.

- Where you'll be a year from now, five years from now, ten years from now, will be the direct result of the decisions that you make from today forward.

- Blaming others is a bad habit, a waste of time, and a cowardly cop-out. Don't do it. If you attract anyone playing that game it will only be whiners, thus furthering your misery.

And here, a favorite quote I first saw in Dan Kennedy's book, *No B.S. Wealth Attraction for Entrepreneurs* (First Edition), which recounts a discussion between Jack Canfield, of *Chicken Soup for the Soul* fame, and W. Clement Stone, a self-made multi-million-aire, where after Stone asks Canfield whether Canfield takes one hundred percent full responsibility for his actions, and Canfield *equivocates*, Stone says:

> If you want to be truly successful, and I know you do, you will have to give up blaming and complaining and take total responsibility for your life...[T]his is a prerequisite for creating a life of success...because if you realize that you have created your own conditions, then you can uncreate them and recreate them at will.

Looking back, I guess it was my parents who first instilled in me—instilled in all of my siblings—the belief that you work your hardest, you do your best, and you never, ever blame anyone else for your situation, even if it was *their* fault. Taking responsibility is the power position.

And they were right, of course.

In every situation you can come up with, for every excuse you can think of, I can point to someone else who's suffered through the same thing and not only survived, but thrived. The most successful people I know default to taking responsibility when crap happens.

Bo Amato, one of the most successful youth and high school soccer coaches in our area, tells his players that if they think the referee made a mistake, it's their fault for not working harder in the first place. Their lack of effort made the referee's job harder.

Only losers point their fingers at "inept" judges, "greedy" insurance companies, and "obnoxious" clients as their reasons for their lack of success. Do we run into bad judges and asshole lawyers? Yes, we do. How do I and my team deal with them? We have a default mindset that says, "You'd be that way too if you lived a life of abject misery like he does. Can you imagine being him?" This changes the way you respond.

Go ahead, make this sign for your bathroom mirror:

YOU can create your own life.

YOU can decide what path you're going to take.

YOU can decide how everything plays out. (Even though it might not always play out to your liking.)

And the Blame Game never, ever has to be played in the process.

. . .

Make No Mistake about It, The Fear of Starting My Own Practice was Real

As I mentioned earlier, the legal part was pretty strong in the firm I was leaving. I was getting good verdicts and healthy settlements. I was enjoying a steady stream of new clients, and I worked hard at making sure my clients were happy, too.

I've already told you about the frustrations that were building at my old firm over the combination of the commute coupled with the general disinterest in doing anything "outside the box" in order to build a real business. Yes, Sandi and I prioritized family relationships over everything else, but that didn't make leaving a good partnership income for a startup easy!

The conversations I was having with Sandi were deep. There was risk to be considered. We had that big mortgage and four children. We knew that we "didn't know what we didn't know" about running a business.

As always, Sandi was (and is) my sounding board and my best friend. The early discussions were tense. This was venturing into the unknown. A few of my friends had started their own firms. Some had flamed out. One got divorced, I am convinced, because his new firm was more stressful than the firm he left. Another ended up quitting the law entirely. Still, there were others who were happy with the decisions they had made about leaving established firms for their own venture.

I'd come home from soccer practice at the end of a long day and say to her, "You know, I'm a good lawyer. I think I might be able to strike out on my own and do this thing by myself."

My decision-making was not instant. It wasn't, "Think about leaving on Friday, move Saturday, and open for business on Monday." But, after many late nights of discussion and prayer, Sandi agreed that we would make the move.

And eventually, it was my own positive "internal self-talk" (my term), combined with Sandi's constant encouragement and ultimate "go ahead," that finally gave me the courage I needed to make the move.

. . .

So Why Am I Standing in the Middle of Office Depot on a Weekday?

Decision made.

Move accomplished.

Then, fear.

Once I actually started my own firm, the fear factor was very high. Really. Shorter commute, yes. Paycheck? Nope. Not one that was guaranteed, anyway.

But Sandi and I were smart. We didn't go out and borrow a whole bunch of money from a bank. We just signed up for every credit card we could get our hands on! A big stack of them.

Yup. We were "smart."

Fortunately, one of my buddies had some extra office space, which meant I had a roof over my head and I could announce to the world, "I am my own boss." Whoopee!

Next stop: Office Depot!

I clearly remember walking through that store with my credit card in hand, looking for paper, a printer, a computer, and saying to myself, *What the hell am I doing here, standing at Office Depot in the middle of a workday? What have I done?*

This felt very weird. Not *liberating* weird. Surreal weird.

It took about six weeks to find and move into the 1,100 square foot office on Old Lee Highway in Fairfax that I would end up occupying for the next twenty-three years. When we moved, we got a three-year lease on a place—we were probably paying something like $2,000 dollars a month—and what I remember especially clearly at the very beginning was having to make so many decisions that had nothing to do with the practice of law: I needed a fax machine, phones, a printer, and someone to connect to a "network" for me. Oh, and the Internet was emerging as a force for business. Fortunately, the office was partially furnished, so I had a nice desk, a conference room table, and chairs to get started.

I clearly remember thinking, *There has got to be somebody out there who I could bring in for sixty or ninety days to help make all these decisions and get me out of this process.*

Fortunately for me, my sister Terry, who'd also been my secretary at the old firm, came over with me. So we left as a team. A *good* team, too. Terry was invaluable to me during that time; she kept me on track and she kept the office running smoothly while I worked on the few cases we had and tried to figure out how we were going to get more.

But at the very beginning, in those first days, I felt almost overwhelmed by all of these new business decisions that had to be made, because I never really had to consider them before.

My old self would tell my young self that when you start your own office, even if you don't have a lot of money:

As much as you can, outsource the things you're not good at. There are plenty of experts, in every conceivable area, who know a lot about the things you know nothing about. Hire them. You don't need to do every single thing yourself. It's exhausting, inefficient, and it prevents you from focusing on your business. If you're spending time figuring out how to run a postage meter, you're not making money. Learn to leverage other people's knowledge. Even if you can only afford a few hours of their time.

And here again, the importance of being a forever learner: One of the first things I did in those early days was take a class in website building; this was around the spring of 1996, and I'm at Erol's—remember Erol's?

Well, before Erol's was a video store, it was a computer company.

So I took this class at Erol's and built my first law firm website. I was now a web developer too!

Even today, in my current office, I still have that very first business announcement. Remember when the Internet was first gearing up and everyone was trying to get ahead of it (or at least keep pace with it) and email addresses were a series of numbers? Mine was 71261.1022@compuserve.com.

There weren't a whole lot of lawyers to send emails to back then, but my business card was impressive because I had an email address.

What is Your "Why?"

My new practice took a long time to gain traction. My new firm had no overarching "reason for being." (Remember, I went in search of a shorter commute.)

You will be able to shortcut your path to success for your law firm the sooner you ask and answer these three questions:

- Why does my firm *deserve* a place in the market?

- How is my practice different from every one of my competitors?

- What is my purpose?

I know that this sounds "airy-fairy," especially if you have started a law firm in order to get a shorter commute (or some other really practical reason, like you hate the people you are working with now), but I can tell you that figuring out answers to these questions and then living them will benefit you enormously.

The answers to these questions not only propel you out of bed each morning, but they will form the basis for your unique marketing message. More on this later.

It took me a long time to articulate a "why" for my firm. I had no mentors encouraging me to think deeply about this. There were no books starting your own law firm (I read them all) that talked about your firm's "purpose." Those books stopped at "This is why you need a good logo," or "Get out there and network," or "Let other lawyers know that you will take the cases that are so bad that they don't want them."

Today we have a clear "why" at Ben Glass Law. It's the thing we feel we are "best in class" at:

> **Ben Glass Law exists to help people make**
> **great decisions about their cases.**

It's not about *we'll get you all the money you deserve* or some fanciful notion of *justice* (seriously, is there an amount of money that someone would trade for severe pain or disability or the death of a loved one?). For us it is this:

> *Something really shitty has happened to your life and you have been thrust into our (legal) world. There are decisions to be made, (including the decision to do nothing at all) and we are going to help you move forward with your life, starting today, by helping you make great decisions.*

> *Period.*

At Ben Glass Law, we live this. It forms the core of everything we do.

If you look at *any* business, in *any* sector, you'll see that those that succeed are the ones who figure this stuff out. Who understand the origin and the intent of their "why." Who realize (and actually live) the basis for their *being*.

All of this might sound a little hazy, a little more hocus-pocus than hard-hitting fact (*especially* if you're considering launching your own firm or completely realigning the priorities and principles of your practice, which is definitely serious business), but you'll need to trust me on this: Figuring out your "why" should be the first and foremost priority.

The rest will flow from there.

> *WARNING: These are concepts that law schools do not teach or even touch. In fact, the law profession old guard does not want lawyers thinking this way at all because it puts you first and that offends some.*

But back to the "why."

I mentioned in an earlier chapter the importance of creating your own life—whatever life that might be—and being unafraid (and unapologetic) about going after the life you choose. But before you start that journey, lay your foundation. If you are well into your journey, remember this: the best time to have thought about this was before you began. The second best time to think about it is right now.

Because the most important element of your foundation is *the why* . . . which is more important than *the how*. The how, as I will demonstrate later in this book, is relatively easy if you have the right leader.

Final note on the "why:" It does you no good to keep your why to yourself. Your team must be in deep alignment with your firm's why. You must hire and fire to the "why." If you find people on your team who do not truly share this value, fire them. Today. (Dan Kennedy's book, *No. B.S. Ruthless Management of People and Profits,* is a good read on this subject.)

To Reach the Goal, Go All-In

Say you've finally figured out your "why."

Now you must take the next necessary step:

Implement it. Which means, live by it.

Which means, align your thinking and your behavior around it.

To make all of this happen, realize that *complete buy-in will be key.*

If you practice the principles of GLM, if you follow the steps we outline for you, there is almost no way you can *not* be successful at achieving goals for your firm and your life.

Let me use another example:

Say you want to lose 25 pounds.

You're not quite sure how to do it, but you know someone who is. You know someone who has the blueprint that will get you all the way there. You also know that if you adhere to this blueprint one hundred percent of the time—if you take every step and follow every footprint—you will get to your goal.

So you start embracing the plan and exercising more and watching those carbs and drinking more water . . . and the weight starts to drop.

But suddenly, you encounter a slight problem. A small snag.

CHOCOLATE CAKE.

Still, you try to stick with the plan. But instead of leaving the cake in the kitchen (or better yet, in the grocery store where it belongs), you develop the pattern of push-ups in the morning . . . and chocolate cake in the evening.

That won't work.

If you're going to lose the weight, you've got to go all in.

But hold on: There's a happy ending to this story.

So you leave the cake alone. You get back to your fitness (CrossFit® for me). You practice total buy-in to the plan.

And gradually, something else begins to happen. (And that "something" definitely does not involved chocolate cake.)

You reach your goal.

Here's my point:

What you want from your practice, what you need from your life, the discovery of your "why," *all of it*, is up to you. But you've got to go all in.

This is your story. This is your one life.

YOU are the author of the next chapter of your life, no one else.

So GLM lawyers are attorneys, obviously—but in a figurative sense, they are authors, too. Because they know that the story they write belongs to them and them alone. They decide.

No one else.

What is good for me and my practice may not be right for you. I would go crazy with thousands of small personal injury cases, but we have members who feast on that type of a practice because it is perfect for their lives. I could not handle the incessant phone calls of distressed parents who are fighting over the kids in a divorce, but if that's you, and you want more of that, then we can help you get there.

I give lawyers the recipe, but they have to first decide what kind of meal they are creating. Creating a firm that serves you first is not all that difficult if you know what you are doing and if you *stop* listening to the naysayers living in the past and the guru of the week who smells blood when he looks at the lawyer market.

. . .

A quick aside here: Running a law firm is not for everyone. It takes a certain amount of ambition (okay, it takes a lot of ambition) to do the hard work necessary to run a firm. Most small businesses, including law firms, fail. Most lawyers are satisfied with where they are. Some are fine with working for someone else. I want to be clear that there is nothing wrong with that. If staying exactly where you are, financially and otherwise, is done by deliberate choice, then who can criticize that choice? Not me.

But please don't whine about the choices you have made. Remember: *deliberate choice.*

It's the lawyers who *want* more/better but who are *unwilling* to apply themselves to that goal who frustrate me (and, I'm sure their children and spouses as well).

Either you're working for somebody else or you have your own practice.

Neither is the "wrong" choice, but there is no in-between.

. . .

"But Ben, my law partner doesn't like your style of marketing."

Here's another thing we hear a lot of: Plenty of lawyers come to GLM events and read my books and they *want* to get their arms around the program, but they can't get the necessary buy-in and support from their colleagues or partners.

I've heard so many lawyers say to me, "I love your stuff! But I can't get my partners to do any of it!"

This is a problem of your own making and it is a solvable problem. Our experience is that it is very difficult to move someone to action who is philosophically opposed to the whole "build a practice that serves you first" idea.

That's fine. I spend little time trying to convince someone they are wrong. I don't have time for those types of discussions. There are plenty of lawyers out there, every day, who come to us wanting to get started.

We are busy.

Here's what usually happens to a lawyer who does find me interesting and who wants to break free of a partner still enamored with yesteryear: they eventually do what I did—they leave and start their own practices. Their first call after telling their old firm they are leaving is often to us: "How do I get started?" I've coached many lawyers through the process of leaving their firm to start out on their own.

Let me say this again: Be your own author.

Entrepreneurial Seizures and Systems

A seizure is a sudden electric event in your brain that totally debilitates you—hopefully, for only a brief period of time. Then you get through it. The concept of *entrepreneurial seizure* is pretty much the same thing.

Michael Gerber, the bestselling author and renowned small business evolutionary, coined the term "E-Myth" in a series of books for entrepreneurs. Gerber's primary thesis is that you should always be building systems in your business that would permit the business to be franchised and then run by others.

Gerber's theory, of course, can be customized to fit any occupation or field at all. Even law.

This is an entrepreneurial seizure: Thinking, I *am a good lawyer, I can run a law firm,* and then just starting a law firm. In Gerber's original book, he tells this story through the eyes of Sarah, a good cake baker who opens a bakery. If you've never read the book, please put it on your list. Yes, I know, you aren't a baker. You are a lawyer. The myth, of course, is thinking that being good at the "doing" of the thing (baking cakes, writing briefs) means that you will be good at running a business involving your "thing."

There is virtually no correlation. Your skill set must be much broader than "good lawyer" in order to run a business. It's helpful, sure, to be a good lawyer, but it is more important to be good at business. You can find a good lawyer anywhere. Business-building experts are hard to find. Sadly, there are many good lawyers who are poor and miserable.

I would sum up the main ideas that run through Gerber's works to be this: Create systems in your business that free you up to do what you are paid to do. Think creatively about solutions to your clients' legal problems. Be the chief strategist for your client. That is your primary job. You do this by creating systems that can be followed by anyone. The better your systems are and the more of them that you have to handle the routine day-to-day activities of your law firm, the more time you free up for thinking.

I do want to make this point: A good lawyer *can* learn to be a good businessperson, but it is hard without a good guide. The two brains are different and you have been told, over and over, to improve the lawyer brain because "if you do good work, they will come." You have spent your entire professional life developing your lawyer brain.

Okay, so that got you where you are today.

Question: Are you happy?

Three of the Worst Words? "We Lost Again"

There were many times after I started my own practice that I was not happy. Anguished would be more like it, on many days.

I remember those times, after having lost a trial, coming home to Sandi, driving up the driveway, parking in my garage, getting out of the car, and Sandi, knowing I had been in trial, opening the door in anticipation.

Immediately she could tell, by the look on my face, whether we won or lost.

With one glance, she'd know. She didn't even have to ask. "We lost again."

I remember feeling real fear during those times; real anxiety. Total helplessness.

How are we going to survive? What are we going to do now? How will we be able to press forward?

Here's the answer to those questions: *What you're going to do is get back up. Move to the next case. Staying down is not an option. Learn to ask: where is the learning in this?*

Balancing the "win-lose" extremes is one of the most difficult tasks we have to master. Lawyers cannot allow themselves to get too sucked in either way. We can't wallow in our losses when we lose and we shouldn't become too euphoric when we win. (At *least* set a time limit for yourself!)

Maintaining this balance is especially difficult, though, for young lawyers who are just starting out and who may have new marriages, small children, tons of debt, and fresh-out-of-law-school careers.

But the good news is that being able to achieve this balance will come, with experience and in time. The more cases you win, the more easily you will be able to balance on that tightrope and straddle between the extremes. And you never win unless you try.

Early in my young entrepreneurial venture I remember trying a malpractice case and losing it. It was gut-wrenching stuff; highly emotional. To make matters worse, no paycheck, a pissed-off client and a ton of case expenses came out of all that pain.

I went on a long run in the rain that afternoon. A long, mindless run to exhaustion. This was years ago, but I remember the run clearly. Somehow I was able to put that afternoon's loss out of my mind during the run. Exercise has always helped me in that way. As one of my CrossFit® buddies said to me recently, "Exercise is my time to be selfish and it always helps."

I got up. Dusted off. Got ready for the next one

Fast-forward two weeks later: I had another trial, another case, against a deputy sheriff, and the jury ended up awarding us $375,000. Sure, it felt great and Sandi and I were euphoric.

However, we'd also learned to ride the wave of the extremes, whichever way it went—and then run back onto that field. Stay in that game. Requesting a substitute to come in and take your place is not an option. (Thanks again, Dad.)

So a variety of factors influenced my decision to start my own law firm; they just happened to converge at pretty much the same time.

I do believe it was God—and my beautiful, brilliant wife Sandi—who helped me weave all of the pieces together in a way that would form the fabric of the rest of my life.

Here, a short list of the factors that finally pushed me towards the creation of my own firm:

1. My need to put my family first (plus, the commute was cruel and unusual punishment).

2. The strength of my abilities and my solid reputation (being a good lawyer gave me the confidence I needed to strike out on my own).

3. The understanding that I wanted (and needed) to create my own life (I knew I had options; I just had to decide which path to take).

4. The courage to do it (if you can call it courage).

These were the factors that pushed me towards the finish line—or maybe I should say *the starting line*, since that's really what it was.

It's the starting line.

It's a decision. Your decision.

How do you start a law firm?

By starting a law firm.

After all, how hard could it be?

CHAPTER FIVE

MY MOST IMPORTANT BELIEF: FAMILY FIRST
EVERYTHING ELSE FLOWS FROM THERE.

What Started it All: A Car and a Key Chain

Thank God I had a car.

My life in college—William & Mary in Williamsburg, Virginia—was a slice out of Americana.

America in the 1970s, I should add.

Classic rock. Drinking age of eighteen. Live music every Wednesday night at the pub (with pitchers of beer, of course). Playing Division I soccer. Lots of horsing around, having fun. Living life.

I first met Sandi when I was a college sophomore. She was a freshman.

I knew her name before I even knew *her*. When I first saw her, she was sitting at a table with some of her friends and I remember she had this big keychain with her name on it.

To this day, I am grateful for that crazy key chain. Why? Because it gave me a leg up: It not only revealed her name to me before we were even introduced, but it helped me *remember* it too, which came in handy when I saw her again.

Sandi was gorgeous (still is). From the minute I saw her, I was drawn to everything about her (still am). It was love at first sight (still is).

I was playing soccer on scholarship for William & Mary, in Williamsburg, Virginia. I also had a job as a referee (no surprise there). I was driving all over the Tidewater region to referee games, so I needed a car.

I think she was impressed by the fact that I had a car. Nobody else was allowed to have one on campus unless you had a "job," but since I was a referee, I needed one, ahem, *"for my work."*

Very important stuff.

So here's another place in the book where I get to say thank you—although this time, I'm not thanking a person . . . I'm thanking a thing.

Two things, really: A keychain and a car.

Without both of them, I would not be *precisely* where I am today. So although this is going to sound a little crazy, I'm doing it anyway. (Plus, when will I ever have another chance?)

To Sandi's key chain and to my first car: *Thank you!*

It's just something that needs to be said.

· · ·

Well, wait.

I need to say thank you again—this time, not to two inanimate objects, but to one human being named Kip Germain, my college buddy and longtime friend who fixed Sandi and me up on our first date.

So I'm telling the story, Kip, this time from my perspective. (He'll know what I mean.)

Kip liked Sandi's roommate, Joan—but he could also tell I was attracted to Sandi. So eventually he comes up with an idea: A double date.

I liked the idea because I was a really shy guy. (A word to Kip: I was planning on asking her out soon, I really was!)

A day or two later, we're all sitting together. Sandi and Joan are there, too. So Kip sees his window of opportunity and goes in for the kill (the way he tells it).

"Hey Sandi," Kip says (always the man with the plan), "why don't you go out with Ben and I'll go out with Joanie and we'll head to the pub on Wednesday night?"

Just that quickly, Kip had stepped in and created the momentum I needed.

The deed had been done. She said yes.

There's even a teachable moment in this:

If you want something to happen, find a way to
MAKE IT HAPPEN. Create the opportunity.

Okay, so in this case it was Kip who "made it happen," which was fine with me. In fact, it was a better option, because I might have chickened out.

So even today, the joke among the three of us is that Kip asked Sandi out on a date for me, and today Kip takes credit for my entire family!

That's fine with me, too, because I'm the one who ended up with the ultimate prize.

Thanks again, Kip.

"Never Again"

Sandi and I have been together ever since. We were married in a Lutheran church by a Lutheran pastor and a Catholic priest. Our reception was in a small firehouse in New Jersey. She had just graduated from college and I had finished my first year of law school.

Life expanded pretty quickly. We had four children in about nine years.

I graduated from George Mason University School of Law in May 1983. Our first child, Brian, was born a few months later, in August. I took the bar in July 1983, which means Brian came into the world before we even knew if I had passed the test to be an attorney.

Things felt like they were a little up in the air. I guess that's because at that particular time in our lives, things *were* up in the air.

This very fact alone caused a certain amount of stress: I *wanted* to be a lawyer because I'd decided long ago it was what I wanted to do with my life, but I *needed* to be a lawyer, too, because we certainly needed the steady income!

Sandi was making about $11,000 a year at that time, which wasn't a ton, but hell, I was going to be a lawyer! We lived in a small one-bedroom apartment in Alexandria. Date nights were to McDonald's. When Sandi's parents would visit, they would sleep on our couch. (And no, it was not one of those pull-out sleep sofas. That would come much later.) We didn't stress about our lives much. Maybe we should have, baby and all, but we didn't. We were living the dream!

Brian, of course, was the joy of our lives.

Even at that early stage, when we only had Brian (oh, how things have changed!), I knew that my family was my number one priority. From the very beginning, then, knowing that *family comes first* is what kept me focused. This is what would help me build my business, grow my practice, and create the kind of life I wanted for myself.

Sandi, who was working as an administrative assistant for a government contractor in Northern Virginia, took off for maternity leave, of course. But when her leave came to an end, we both faced growing trepidation about handing Brian over to someone else who'd care for him during the day.

I know, I know. Just about every young couple with a new child faces these same fears. Nothing new there. In fact, knowing that we were not alone—knowing that every new parent must face this same anxiety—is what gave us a small measure of comfort—but not all that much.

So we soldiered through the anxiety and on that first day of daycare, we delivered our son to this lady in an apartment complex. (I forget how we even found her.) She was taking care of other kids too—babies and infants—and we both had a sick feeling about the whole thing. It was just really hard for us.

I'm certainly not saying that it's *bad* for parents to rely on daycare—millions of other responsible working parents do—but it just wasn't for us.

Even though we didn't want to become overreactive new parents, dropping him off at that apartment complex was more than we could handle.

Sandi and I both agreed at the end of day one: "Nope. Never again. Not going to do this."

Never again would we leave our child with a stranger.

And here, a gift from God: My mom stepped in and simply said, "I'll take care of him."

And just like that, our crisis was averted.

So Brian's first babysitter was his grandmother, my mother. And it couldn't have worked out any better.

My mother loved taking care of Brian during the day, and Brian certainly loved the attention and care he received from his grandmother. We couldn't have asked for a better situation.

Those two were quite a pair, and Mom was the greatest grandmother in the world. We trusted her with everything we had. We loved her in every way we knew how. And we appreciated everything she did. We always will.

. . .

Throughout this book I've emphasized (overemphasized might be the better word) the importance of creating your own reality. And I'm about to do it again here. I don't really care if it sounds repetitive: I need to make the point again, except this time, it has a little bit of a twist.

In addition to creating your own reality, it's important to recognize and appreciate the fact that people around you can be instrumental in helping you achieve that mission, too. **Although you are the ultimate author of your own story, the people around who love you and want to see you happy in your life can also help write the words.**

In our busy lives, we *forget* that sometimes.

So here, a two-part teachable moment. You should always try to:

1. Create your own reality

2. Remember to recognize and appreciate the people around you who help guide you to that goal, too.

Children and teenagers can be forgiven for not appreciating the influence that others have on their lives. You are an adult. You have no excuse. If there is someone in your life who, no matter how long ago, did something to help you move forward on your journey, today would be a good time to give that person a call or write them a note. Not email. Not text. Use real paper. A real stamp.

The Call to Adopt

One day quite a few years later—four children later, to be exact—Sandi came up to me and made a simple statement:

"I think I'm being called to adopt a child."

I said, "You're crazy. We already have four kids and a dog. Our lives are filled up. We have no more to give."

For me, the idea quickly passed. But Sandi knew it—as Sandi knows everything—with certainty and conviction. She and God were hatching a plan.

One day, my daughter Caitlin, then in high school (and now a pastor), invited Sandi and me to a Christian rock concert she and some friends were going to.

We didn't know one thing about Christian rock; we'd barely even heard of it. But we didn't have anything else to do on that Saturday night, so we simply answered, "Okay, we'll go!"

It was a Steven Curtis Chapman concert. If you've been to one, you can probably guess what's coming.

Friday, March 8, 2002, changed the trajectory of our lives.

We'd never seen Steven Curtis Chapman perform before. Never heard anything about him. I didn't recognize his name and hadn't heard any of his songs. I also didn't know he had a song "When Love Takes You In." But his performance that night during his "Live Out Loud" tour at Hylton Memorial Chapel in Dale City, Virginia, changed my heart. During the concert he was advocating for supporting orphans—not necessarily adopting them, but simply offering monetary support.

As we listened to Chapman speak and sing and touch the audience in a way I'd never been touched before, I clearly felt that God was speaking directly to me. As I sat in the audience, I openly wept at the enormity of the "ask" I felt God was making of us.

At church two days later, I told my pastor, Tom Bailey, "I don't know if you've ever had an actual religious experience before, but I think I did two nights ago."

The experience had completely altered my life and expanded my heart. Sandi had already received the calling.

One concert. One night. One random "yes" to the invitation from Caitlin.

Coincidence? I think not. God was speaking to us both.

Seventeen months later, Sandi and I were on a flight traveling to Guanxi Province in southern China on our way to adopt Kevin, who was eighteen months old.

But before that, more fear.

After the concert, I had given Sandi the go-ahead to begin the adoption process in earnest. At this point our youngest biological child, Matt, was two years old. We began attending adoption seminars, reading books, and asking questions. The adoption process is complex on so many levels. We talked to different adoption agencies. There were so many choices to make: domestic or international? If international, which country? Special needs or non-special needs; boy or girl; adopt in birth order, or not? Once again, we didn't know what we didn't know.

At times we waivered in our "yes." What were we thinking? Even though they wouldn't say it to our faces, some thought we were crazy. We made lists of pros and cons.

Again, God spoke to us.

It was one Sunday morning and we were stressing over the decision to adopt. We hadn't told anyone about our self-doubt but there we were, sitting in church, having worked on yet another pro and con list the day before, when Pastor Bailey gave a sermon on fear. He talked about St. Peter walking on the stormy sea water towards Jesus, wanting to have faith but not believing he could do it, and feeling like he was going to sink. Without knowing that on that morning our list was tilted toward "no," he asked the congregation, "What would you do if you knew you would not fail? If you want to make a difference, sometimes you have to step out of the boat and onto the water."

Once again, I wept. This time Sandi joined me, sobbing silently, as we both felt that again God was speaking directly to us, answering our questions and prayers.

We eventually narrowed our choice to "special needs, China." We knew there were many couples who, not being able to conceive, were in line to adopt a non-special needs child (at that time, usually a girl) from China. Already blessed with five children, we did not want to slow down the process for those couples, so we got in the "special needs" line.

Once we chose an agency with experience in China, we began to explore pictures and profiles of children who were waiting for their "forever families." One evening, I was out of town taking depositions when Sandi sent me an email with a link to our future son Kevin's info. That night, we both knew that Kevin was meant to be a part of our family.

Kevin was born with a cleft lip and palette and, unlike most babies born in the United States with a cleft, his had never been repaired—I'd never seen one before and could not imagine how you eat and live with an unrepaired cleft. Truth is, like Kevin, you don't eat very well. It takes time to feed a child with a cleft. They didn't always have time in a crowded orphanage in southern China. This still wasn't a deterrent for us—we trusted God completely and, after a lot of research about the condition and discussion with experts, knew with total confidence that we were going to move forward.

And here, I need to thank my sister, Terry Patterson, for showing us, in her own life, that an adoption like this can unfold. She and her husband had already adopted their first child from China.

Kevin became our sixth child. And the reason we loved him like our own is because he *was* our own. People ask, "Is there any difference in feelings toward an adoptive child versus your biological children?" The answer is no. I can't explain that fully, but from the moment we said yes to God about Kevin, he was "ours" even though he was still a world away from us.

We are all the same.

As I was finishing up this manuscript, Kevin was starting his junior year in high school.

Still Standing

About eighteen months later, Sandi comes to me and says, "I think I'm being called again to adopt. I think there's a little girl in China who needs a home. Come see what's on my computer monitor."

This time around, I didn't think she was that crazy. Not even for a minute. I accepted it fully and completely. Besides, I was powerless to say no to God *and* to Sandi.

This time, the photo from the adoption agency showed a little five-year-old girl who was missing several fingers on each hand. While she was then in an orphanage, she had spent significant time with a foster family in China.

"Ben, meet Emma, your next daughter," God said to me.

Emma was born in July 2000, in the Shandong province, China.

She was six when we finally met her in person. This was a different experience from Kevin because she was older. We really didn't know what to expect. She had experienced the world a bit and her missing fingers had had little impact on her development.

Emma didn't like me when we first met. Not only was I a stranger, but I was a man and she had not had any adult men in her life. She was impish and funny, right from the beginning, though. This little girl who had just met us would take our camera, pretend to photograph Sandi and me together in front of some historic site in China, only to find out later that she had cropped me out of the picture. She found that to be hilarious.

We returned to the United States and Emma jumped right into school in kindergarten, even though she knew no English. As I was finishing up the writing of this book, she was getting ready to graduate high school and head off to Virginia Tech, where her brother, Matt, is already in school to study neuroscience.

God was still writing plans for our family. Big plans.

Two years after Emma came home, Sandi called me back into her office to look at her computer screen again. "There's a group advocating for older children adoption in China. If a child turns fourteen, they are no longer eligible for adoption. They will remain in the Chinese social welfare system until they are older, but they will never be able to leave China. Look at this video."

As I looked over her shoulder, Sandi showed me a video of an eleven-year-old girl and a twelve-year-old boy playing musical chairs in an orphanage. The girl had a repaired cleft lip and palette, the young man was missing an ear. They appeared happy and joyful. They were available for adoption.

Another new experience: Older child adoptions can prove to be challenging beyond any obvious "special need." Years and years in an orphanage changes the wiring of your brain.

God was reminding us that children of *every* age, not just infants, need safe and loving homes. He was asking Sandi and me to stretch once again. This time our answer was not immediate. We had a large family of seven children by then. China had rules against adopting two children at once. David and Leah would be well out of birth order in our family. We started doing college tuition math in our heads.

More praying, investigation, and deep thought this time, before our yes to God and to these children, but yes was the answer that we gave.

People will say to us, "You are brave and courageous and you have done a great thing, 'saving' these children."

It's not that way at all. When David and Leah agreed to become our children (since they were twelve and eleven at the time, they had to consent to the adoption process) they were agreeing to leave their language, their culture, their friends—everything they knew—in order to get on a plane to travel with people they didn't know to a land they knew little about. More than that, David remembers being taught that America was an evil place, "where everyone carries guns and they fly planes into buildings."

Even though it may seem like every child living in a foreign orphanage would immediately choose to leave what they know to come live with a family in America, this is not the case at all. This is a big decision for everyone.

Both Leah and David were born in Beijing; Leah came into the world in August 1998 and David in April 1997. On those dates, too, our trajectory shifted and our world changed, though we didn't know it at the time.

How brave these children were! What most people don't understand is how much richer our lives are because of the adoption experience. We've met great friends and professionals who we would never have encountered in our lives, people who are living their lives "out loud." We have watched all our children grow immensely. As I am finishing this book, Leah has graduated high school and is working and David is entering his third year at

George Mason University.

Here is the rest of the "lineup." Brian has three boys and is an attorney at Ben Glass Law; Caitlin has one daughter and is a Lutheran pastor; Patrick is a firefighter and paramedic and served with the U.S. Army in Afghanistan; Kelsey is a first-grade teacher; and Matt, as I noted above, is studying business at Virginia Tech.

"Forever Learning" Works with Family, Too

Today, our home is filled with all kinds of books, information, and resources about family, child-rearing, "secondary trauma," and what we call "raising kids from hard places."

If it has something to do with adoption or raising kids with special needs or how families face challenges, it's probably in our library.

But it's Sandi, really, who has developed the deepest, widest breadth of knowledge about adoption and raising children who face special challenges. People who are looking for information on these subjects come to her for guidance, information, and support. She's worked hard, over the years, to align herself with the foremost experts in the nation, and in a very real way, she's become one of those experts herself.

> **A note:** *If you are reading this book and are considering adoption or, having adopted, have questions about your new life, feel free to reach out to Sandi and me. We have a lot of experience and can direct you to a lot of resources that are worth study. This is a part of our mission now.*
>
> *We are a family of forever learners.*

Again, this is a perfect example of how gathering as much information as possible on a subject will actually be of great benefit to *all* of the parties involved—not just to Sandi and me, but to our kids, too.

Let's push this example a little further out: Lawyers who feel they aren't getting all they deserve out of their practices search me out all the time. Many make it their business to read everything they can get their hands on about either Ben Glass Law or Great Legal Marketing. And they are right to do it. *Learn as much as you can about the subject you need to know about.* As I tell high school students when I speak to their classes, "If you are struggling with a topic, there is no lack of information out there for anyone who is willing to take the time to track it down."

Now, loop this back to your own practice. Your clients have been thrust into the legal world, often without warning or preparation. They are looking for information, fast. Today, how much free information about the subject of your practice areas do you provide to consumers? I'm not talking about your plaques and awards. They aren't interested in that just yet. They want information. Can they get it from you easily? It's what today's consumers want.

Give it to them. (More about that later.)

AND THEN LEARN MORE.

Raising our own five biological children together with our four adopted from China has been challenging. I won't sugarcoat it: this has, at times, required every ounce of our energy, ingenuity, and patience. This created enormous stress on the marriage, on the family as a unit, and on life in general. There were times when we thought the pressure would tear our family apart. We sometimes felt like "giving up," but there was no "giving up" to be done.

We had to get good at it.

We had to relearn everything we thought we knew about parenting. We had to come up with new ways of doing things; an entirely new and different paradigm for parenting. We had to track down other people who had been through this journey before and tap their brains for answers.

In fact, we didn't just shoulder through the challenges, we were (and are) strengthened by them.

Our large and loving family and the challenges we face each and every day—not just with our adoptive children, but with the entire family unit, since there are so many moving parts—this is what keeps us strong and keeps us together.

I've said in earlier chapters that **THERE IS NOTHING THAT CANNOT BE LEARNED.**

This is true of parenting, too.

Sandi and I were forced to learn a new and completely unorthodox type of parenting because the old ways just didn't work for us when we began raising our adoptive children. But we knew we could do it—and we did. We made it work.

And we still are today.

Here is something else we strongly believe: The traditional, one-size-fits-all "put you in a room and teach you" educational model no longer works. Maybe it never did. Everybody is different. College is not for everyone. Each of our children have different needs, different personalities. Yours too.

If you have a child who learns differently, know this:

- You will get lots of well-meaning advice on your parenting journey. Consider the source and never be shamed into a method that you are not 100 percent comfortable with.

- When you find yourself on a difficult road, know that there are others just ahead of you and some who are far ahead of you. Search for and ask questions of those who have travelled that road and who speak positively about the experience. It does no good to hang out with whiners.

- Parenting works best when both parents are on the same page, philosophically. This means that to be effective you, as a couple, have to fix your own stuff first.

- Do not be afraid to stand up to teachers and school administrators who are not as knowledgeable as you are about whatever diagnosis or challenge your child has. Assuming you have worked hard on becoming educated about the science involved, don't back down.

- If you have a child who has educational challenges, investing in the expertise of the right educational consultant will pay many dividends.

Sandi and I do consider ourselves experts in child-rearing. Nine children makes you an expert. Here are a few lessons from the Glass Family Playbook. I'll go into further detail about these lessons in the next chapter, but for now, consider heeding this advice:

Get Off Their Backs

There is a difference between coaching your kid through life and reliving your own failed childhood. Let them live and let them make mistakes. They need to own the natural consequences of their actions. Are they going to get an F because they left their report at home? It won't kill them to not disrupt your day, get in your car, and rescue them. This will build resilience.

Role Models Matter

Both Sandi and I had terrific role models. Her parents are in a long-running marriage. My parents were married over sixty-seven years when my mother passed away. Your children are watching you. Our children have adult mentors and models at our church. They may not always listen to mom and dad, but if Tom or El Porter whisper in their ear while walking down the halls of Abiding Presence Lutheran Church, their voices have power. This applies to the sports coaches your kids may have, too. If you cringe at the way the coach talks to children, parents or referees, don't just stand there and say nothing. If a coach is not a good role model for your kids and your community, let them know how you feel. If they don't change, move on.

Share Your Fears

Children pick up on your stress. It's okay to say, "Dad is worried about an upcoming case," or "Mom is a little tired right now because the baby stayed up all night." Children need to know that you have things that scare you, too. Teaching your children that it is okay to share their feelings in your home will help them feel secure.

When You Are Wrong, Apologize

Sandi and I argue sometimes. We say inappropriate things to each other in front of the kids. We are human. It's vital that when this happens, we make sure to round back with the children about what happened. Children sometimes have irrational fears about abandonment, divorce, et cetera. It's okay to be open and honest. Children feel the stress of arguing parents. They need to see the apology too.

Stop Lecturing

Do you like getting lectured to? Our experience is that lectures never work. Sure, we might blow off some steam and feel better but it's really not moving a child to better behavior. Modeling good behavior moves children to better behavior. By all means, don't lecture while you and your child are upset. Teach in a time of calm.

Don't Take Your Business Home

I learned very quickly in the game to never take my business and my work home with me. It's not fair to my family. And it's not fair to me.

When I'm home, they deserve one hundred percent of my time, and I expect to be able to give them that. They expect it, too.

This is why putting my family as my first priority stands at the center of everything I do. It gives me balance, too: When I'm at work, I work—and I work hard. But when I'm home, I'm home with my family as a husband and a father.

Got work to do? This is more of a time management problem than anything else. You can start by getting up earlier than anyone else. Like any other habit, this can be learned. (More on getting better control of your time later.)

Make Your Family Your Priority (For Real)

The cohesive family is something we see not just as a necessity but as a *value*. It is about *leadership* and *responsibility*. If you ask lawyers what they value, most will say family. If you follow them around for a week, you will see that they are lying about this.

No matter where you are, you can change and renew.

The disintegration of the family has led to moral decay in America. Life is not meant to be lived alone.

This is not easy. It's HARD. I get it, but the alternative is not acceptable. The National Task Force Report on Lawyer Well-being makes this point very clear. To the extent that we can bring more sanity to our professional lives, we can reduce the stress back at home.

But by putting my family first and keeping them at the center of my vision, I was forced to figure out everything else. It did not happen overnight. The business must serve, not destroy, the family. I am not perfect at it. It can be done. Shame on those who do not even try. Shame on any leader in the legal profession who does anything to hinder those of us who do understand that building a sane, profitable business can have an enormous influence on a lawyer's ability to (really) make family a priority.

You can do it. Thousands of lawyers have taken up the challenge and are on a renewed fight for their families and for their own health. They aren't being led by the established bar, which voices platitudes about "wellness," but then refuses to seriously consider the value of teaching lawyers how to run businesses.

These lawyers are being led by voices like mine, which say, "There has to be another way." Don't let your law practice get in the way of your life.

Repeating Patterns

I certainly didn't plan this when I was developing the outline for this book. And I didn't expect it to emerge as I was writing it, but there's a theme that seems to have emerged in just about every chapter so far that I find kind of interesting.

Life repeats itself. Patterns keep coming up from yesterday that find a way into today; into our present-day lives. For example: My father instilled in me a love of sports and healthy competition. My mother was a gentle soul who made you feel very special, no matter who you were. Both my parents and Sandi's parents instilled in us the kinds of values that we instilled in our own kids, and now, that they are instilling in *their* kids.

What that tells me is that we have to be conscious about how we live our lives. We have to realize that the patterns we create will be repeated—whether it's in your business, in your practice, or in your children.

This makes the concept of "creating your own life" even more important. Why? Because if we know that there's a high likelihood that these patterns will be repeated, we better make sure they're worthy of being repeated. Put simply, what we create in our lives is what we eventually want to pass down.

I'm not much of a philosopher, but I've lived long enough to know this: *Life does come full circle*. And I see this *most* clearly when I look at my own kids.

Every one of them who has launched into the real world has come back to us and said, "We are so thankful that you and Mom raised us the way you did. Giving us space, not demanding perfection, not always pushing us beyond where we wanted to be pushed. Sure, you set boundaries for us, but you let us *live*."

Today we have five grandchildren (at least as of this writing, anyway). They are still very young, but I can already see some patterns emerging.

What's really cool and greatly gratifying is being able to watch how our children are raising *their* children. I'm happy—and very proud—to say that our kids are really good at being parents: I can already see that. They're loving and kind in the same way that Sandi and I were (and still are) to them.

That, to me, is the greatest blessing of all.

SECTION II

THE LESSONS AND THE MISTAKES

CHAPTER SIX
WHAT I WOULD TELL A YOUNG LAWYER RAISING CHILDREN

I f you're raising a family right now or if you're thinking about starting one sometime in the near future, here's the first thing I want to tell you right off the bat: It can be done and you can do it. I should probably add another line to that: Plenty of good lawyers do it every single day.

I wrote those last words to remind you of something important: You won't be the first person to strike the balance between parenting and practicing law, and you won't be the last. Let that be a comfort to you.

Within Great Legal Marketing, we have members in virtually every consumer practice area, from coast to coast and border to border (and beyond) who are not only striking a *comfortable* balance between raising children and practicing law, but are doing it well, determined to not be those people who, while they were scrambling around trying to finish briefs and return calls, *missed watching their children grow up.*

Especially to the younger lawyers who might be new to either practicing or parenting (or maybe even to both), know this up front: It's a lot of hard work, but the payoff is huge. The foundation you create for your children in the first eighteen years of their lives will serve them for the *rest of their lives.*

When you look at it this way, it's easy to understand why being there for your children in their early years is so important: They grow up fast. Every day with your children will be a gift— whether that day is a good day or a crappy day—it's still going to be a gift.

Sure, you'll develop your own parenting path and ultimately decide what works best for you. That's what you *should* do. But it might also be helpful to cherry-pick your way through this chapter in the hopes of coming across a few pieces of advice that might resonate. I am, after all, somewhat of an expert on raising children.

Raising your children will be the most important thing you'll ever do.

Take it from someone who knows.

. . .

If you've read any of the earlier chapters of this book, you already know I'm the father of nine children, five biological and four adopted from China. If you've heard me speak, attended my training sessions, or have already aligned yourself with the principles of GLM, then you also know that my family is my number one priority—and I'm not at all shy about saying it.

My law firm business cards describe me as "Dad to Nine." My marketing features my family at *least* as prominently as it features me. I talk about my children every chance I can get.

Why shouldn't I? The fact that I place them first and foremost is the very reason I'm here today, doing what I do, living the life I live, and it's one of the most important principles of GLM. Don't be that lawyer who says, "I put family first" but then doesn't live it!

I've also described in earlier chapters how Sandi and I had to relearn everything we thought we knew about parenting when we adopted our four children from China, because with these four, the traditional model of parenting was not an option. Early childhood trauma is real and required new thinking.

I can definitely call myself an expert in child raising. Though I do a lot of things—run a successful business and a thriving law firm, teach seminars and workshops to lawyers from all over the country, referee soccer games, practice CrossFit®, the list goes on and on—I know that *being a good father* is what I probably do best. Good thing because it's the most important.

So pick and choose your way through this chapter. Hold onto the advice that you think might work for you and let go of the stuff that doesn't. (Or maybe file it away for later).

I'll tick through them here, hopeful that they will be of some use.

Be Willing to Put in the Work

Our first five biological kids were self-sufficient and pretty typically developed. But raising our four adoptive children required Sandi and me to abandon and relearn everything we thought we knew about parenting. The old model no longer worked.

I also mentioned in the previous chapter how deeply we dove into getting our hands on as much information and as many resources as we possibly could on the subject of raising children with trauma histories. We bought books and CDs, attended seminars, and developed relationships with the experts and gurus who knew what we needed to know about this topic.

Here are our top parenting resources:

EmpoweredToConnect.org—the work of the late Dr. Karyn Purvis. Her book, The Connected Child, should be mandatory reading for all new parents.

BeyondConsequences.com—Sandi and I were so impressed with Heather Forbes that several years ago we invited her to travel across the country to speak at our church.

A Note: *Even though Sandi and I discovered Dr. Purvis and Heather Forbes in our quest for information to help us understand our adoptive children, their books, CDs, and DVDs are applicable to raising all children.*

When it came to our children, we applied the principle of being a forever learner. Today, if you are struggling with raising your children, there is no lack of good resources out there. A major mission for Sandi and me, moving forward, is to be a resource for other parents. Feel free to reach out.

An important lesson here is that we were willing to do whatever was necessary for the good of our children and to ensure the well-being and cohesion of the Glass family unit. Having already identified my family as my number one priority only sharpened my focus on doing whatever I needed to do to help them thrive.

It's a good thing we were so willing, too: After raising five kids using a more traditional parenting model, changing courses midstream to create an *entirely different* parenting model was no easy feat. But we did it. That's a simple way of saying this:

Be willing to change your ways. Every child is different.

They're Watching You!

This won't come as *new news* to anyone, but it's certainly worth re-peating here, especially if you're new to child-rearing:

Your kids are watching you. What you do *matters more than what you say.*

Watch it when you find yourself drifting into lecture mode. What you *tell* your children about how to act and behave in the world isn't really going to matter nearly as much as what you model for them. Yes, they'll "hear" what you're saying and they might even remember it for a little while, but it's not going to stick if your own actions contradict your lectures.

For example, if you're lecturing on the dangers of texting while driving, but on the way home from soccer practice that same day they see you dashing off a quick text while you're waiting for the light to turn green, chances are good that your lecture has been for nothing. Walk the walk.

Here's the soccer field again as the backdrop: On the way to the game, you're giving your thousandth lecture to your young athlete about the importance of good sportsmanship, but during the game they see (and hear) you screaming and arm-waving and causing holy hell on the sidelines about a "bad call" the referee made.

You cannot be that jerk screaming from the sidelines. Not if you're trying to teach your kid that sportsmanship counts.

You also should have your athletes playing only for coaches whose values track yours. Here's an email I sent to one of my son's coaches, Bo Amato, after a game several years ago that involved seventeen- to eighteen-year-olds:

To: Bo Amato
From: Ben Glass

Subject: Sometimes it's good to...

Bo:

I think it's good to have the parents sitting on the same side of the field as the coaches as we did yesterday. Then they can hear you telling the boys to stop whining, be tough, and get on with the game.

Youth soccer is a short term game... at 19 they move on to the rest of life. Some will play in college but most won't.

The message that you send that they must learn to fight through adversity, always try to produce quality, completely ignore refereeing decisions that go against them and get ready for the next play, immediately congratulate their opponents once the game is over no matter what the result, are life lessons.

I think the last 20 minutes of yesterday's final showed the product of your relentless message... that was a fascinating ending to the tournament, with players never giving up, even though there were I think 4 players who by then had picked up knocks that prevented them from going on.

Culture starts at the top. There is a reason you have been so successful.

Thanks,
Ben

Fortunately, each one of my adult children who has gone off into the world has come back and told me how heavily (and favorably) influenced they were by what they saw and heard in our household when they were younger.

Sandi and I are not perfect, but their message was: "We absorbed what we observed, and we are grateful for it."

So practice what you preach. And be consistent with your messaging. An occasional burst of kindness or a random display of compassion every now and then is just not going to cut it. It won't feel believable. *Be kind and compassionate to people all the time.* Our children from "hard places" taught us that last part.

Your kids need you to show them, not just tell them.

Model the behavior you want to see in your family.

It's Okay to be a Jerk . . . with Your Time

What I'm going to say next might sound ridiculously simple, but since we all know that simple does not always mean *easy*, I'm going to say it loud and clear: *To be a good parent, develop good habits.*

On the evenings and the weekends, shut off your phone. Turn off your computer. Put down that brief. Be present for your family. Your children need it, and so do you. For lots of lawyers, this will require the breaking of bad habits: Sleeping with your cell phone at arm's reach (or even under your pillow, and believe me, lots of lawyers have told me they do it) is a bad habit. So are two-hour "call-back guarantees." (Honestly, how does anyone get any quality work done if you are calling everyone back in two hours?)

Learn to make your home time your own time.

Understand this, too: It's not your fault if you believe that making yourself available to your clients 24/7 is a requirement of success or demanded by the profession, because *this is what you have been trained to do.* This is the status quo's definition of being a "good lawyer." It just happens to be off-base, screwed-up, and antithetical to enjoying life.

Here's the way I do it: When I get home to my family, I ditch my cell phone. I don't just put it on mute, I turn it off. I don't even give it *a chance* to become a distraction. I don't have email on my phone, or Safari or Facebook. None of those whiz-bang apps that claim to make your life easier but only succeed in making it more complicated. Everything (except GPS and the message app) goes off at 7:00 p.m. And turning off these "must-have" apps has not adversely affected my life one bit.[2]

When I'm with my family, I'm with my family. Period.

So a word of advice: Shut down, close up, and turn off all the electronic distractions as soon as you get home. It will really be a life-changer: I promise.

> **A note:** *I'm convinced that the technology we rely on today is just as addictive as nicotine, cocaine, or heroin. (Maybe even more so because we've been tricked into thinking that the more we use it, the more productive we become, which couldn't be further from the truth.) Technology was supposed to free, not enslave us.*

Here's the long and short of it: Get your business in order while you're in the office so that we you come home at night, you can be present for your family.

Learn to be a jerk with your time. When you're home with your family, *be home* with your family. Those sending you emails on Saturday can wait. You have a Little League Baseball game to watch.

Be present.

---

2. Cal Newport has written two must-read books on this topic. Both *Deep Work* and *Digital Minimalism* are on my list of books to read *annually.*

Ask Questions to Understand, Not to Argue

When you're having a conversation with someone who disagrees with you, it's important to learn *not* how to argue, but how to ask good questions. Asking good questions, having a genuine desire to understand the other person and get to the root of their beliefs, not only makes life more interesting, it can also help mold and influence how you might feel about the issue. Plus, arguing with someone only pisses you both off. Asking great questions requires discipline and you will either prove that you are correct by your questions or you will learn something by the answers you get.

This is an important skill to teach your children—how to ask questions in a way that really allows both people to hone in on the root core of a disagreement. Asking questions requires you to listen to the answer before asking the next question. Listen, ask. Listen, ask. Listen, ask.

This is a high-level cognitive skill. Help your kids develop the skill of asking good questions; help them internalize this way of communicating with someone with whom they disagree. It was how we communicated around the dinner table just about every night of the week: by asking each other good questions.

My twenty-year-old son David, now a student at George Mason University (I'd describe it as, like most universities, a liberal university), came to the U.S. from China when he was twelve years old. He has lived under Communism. He knows the difference between liberty and tyranny.

David, who's very interested in politics and government and is a conservative thinker, often gets into lengthy discussions with his classmates. He's told me on a couple of occasions that his buddies often get frustrated by his insightful questions that are nothing more than his attempt to understand the basis for their views. Most, it turns out, can't articulate any rational basis for their beliefs once they get past the headline, and that is frustrating to them as he asks deeper and better questions. What they don't realize is that he's not asking them questions to "prove" his agenda—he is genuinely curious. This is the way we raised him. It's an important skill for any young person to develop.

Once, after taking a first-year philosophy class, he came home and said, "Dad, we're reading about this guy named Socrates and he sounds just like you! He never argued with anybody, he just kept asking really good questions, and this is how he learned!"

And then David said something that made us smile. "That's exactly what you used to do with us at the dinner table when we were growing up! It was frustrating to have to keep defending the beliefs I thought I had but it made me learn to think more deeply about the issues."

Let's take a quick detour and look at the larger link to business. Business owners don't need to know the answers to every single question. They just need to know how to ask deeper and better questions to get the information they need in order to make the right decision or find the best solution.

We made it a priority to teach our kids this skill *when they were kids*. And it's helpful to them now, in their adult lives.

Teach your kids how to ask good questions.

Play Multiple Sports

This lesson is simple and straightforward: Let your kids be kids.

When they're in school, don't pigeonhole your child into playing one sport and one sport only. It's not fair to him and it limits his overall development. Every college coach I've ever talked to has agreed: Coaches are looking for strong, well-rounded athletes who've played multiple sports. Don't get hung up on getting your kid onto a travel team when he's eight or nine years old. It's a trap. It's also ridiculous. (I had one dad tell me that his eight-year-old had been "identified" by his child's recreational soccer club to be "promoted" to the travel team to be coached by "specialists." This crap starts by brainwashing the parents.)

I'll say it again: Let your nine-year-old be a nine-year-old instead of a travel team star. He'll thank you for it later. (I know mine did.)

My son Matt played soccer in school, but he didn't even *start* in travel soccer until he was thirteen. Sure, by the time he graduated high school he'd become a strong travel team player, but well before that he played seasonal sports: Basketball, baseball, recreational soccer. I'm convinced that he eventually became such a strong soccer player because he played a broad-based variety of recreational sports first.

When I was young, as I mentioned at the beginning of the book, we played all kinds of sports, usually right in my backyard. We didn't have any coaches or referees, of course, and we didn't *need* any coaches or referees. We were just kids playing baseball. Or soccer. Or whatever we happened to be playing at any given moment. This was our diversity training.

Lots of times our games even ended up in fights. But the next day, we'd be back out there, starting up all over again. And that was just fine. We were learning life lessons about self-control, establishing boundaries and about not taking sports too seriously.

Another slight detour here, this time making the larger link to both the practice and the study of law: If you are heading off to law school, be diverse in your learning once you get there. Instead of doing law review, which is vastly overrated, you're better off sneaking off to the community college and taking some business courses. I know, I know—radical.

It's more beneficial to you to know at least a little bit about a lot of different subjects, especially if you're going to run a business or start a law firm at some point. If you're just starting out, there's a lot you'll need to know, a lot you'll need to absorb, a lot you'll need to master. Writing some obscure article for law review that no one will ever read once it is published is a waste of time that could be devoted to learning something that will actually advance your life.

But back to the kids: teaching your kids to expand their focus and broaden their interests early in life will put them that much ahead of the game.

Let them play. Let them shout. Let them *live*.

On the field and in life, make sure your kids are well-rounded.

Face Fear

Sandi and I quickly learned that whenever one of our kids overreacted or responded negatively to a situation (and this was particularly true of our adopted children) there was likely an element of *fear* involved.

When a child does something wrong or breaks the rules, they're not *trying* to be rebellious. They're not *trying* to raise hell. Especially to the young parents who are reading this who might not always understand or expect that sudden outburst before a doctor's appointment or that raging temper tantrum on the way to school: know that this behavior is often rooted in fear. Don't take it personally, and don't go directly into an angry or frustrated reactive mode.

Instead, *let it cause you to pause.*

In the middle of the meltdown (your kids', not yours) allow yourself an extra second or two to reassess the situation and truly understand that fear is the factor, not obstinance. This is something Sandi and I had to learn; it's something that we studied carefully.

This is very outside-the-box thinking, not at all the traditional model of parenting, and it has worked for us. In fact, the "pause" really helped us maintain our *own* sanity.

Here's the lesson about fear that can be used in the larger world of lawyering: when you run into a client (or a potential client) who's a real jerk, let your default be, "There's stuff going on in his life that isn't good and he's probably acting like this because he's afraid."

That doesn't let him off the hook, by any means, nor does it make him any less of a jerk. By understanding that the motivating factor is usually fear, it helps you diffuse the situation and view things through a wider prism.

Every lawyer who reads this knows the challenges of dealing with a difficult client. In fact, it's one of the reasons lawyers are so stressed out all the time. But there's a way to diffuse the stress.

At Ben Glass Law, we try very hard to understand (and remember) that every client who walks through that door is there because *something has gone wrong in their life, they're frightened about it,* and they are turning to us to help them figure out how to fix it.

I often make the joke that, "People don't come into my office to say, 'Here, I need your help with spending all of my lottery winnings.'" They don't *enjoy* paying someone else to help them get through a crisis. They're usually scared.

And they're scared because something pretty awful has usually happened in their lives.

This is an essential principle to understand, not just in a child's world, but in an adult's, too.

As long as we're on the subject of difficult choices, let me offer this up, because there are really only two choices available for handling a crappy client:

1. You can be equally disagreeable and ill-tempered. (This is never the right option. If your client is eliciting this kind of negative reaction from you, fire him.)

2. You can default to, "I actually feel kind of bad for this person. Something very bad has happened to him that is contributing to this behavior, and maybe I can help sort it out." (Or maybe not. But at least I'm going to try to give the client the benefit of the doubt.)

Part of my job at GLM is to help broaden the scope of a lawyer's knowledge so that it expands beyond, "How do we get more clients" to some pretty interesting philosophical questions about life and about dealing with people. Again, this is stuff they don't teach you in law school and you won't read in any of the other lawyer marketing "how-to" books. The other "gurus" out there selling marketing and coaching advice don't understand it either since they aren't meeting any law clients, ever.

So at any level and in any circumstance—with your children, in your practice, even in law school—fear can be faced, and it can be understood. And while this doesn't *excuse* the bad behavior, it certainly might help *explain* it.

Understand that your child's unruly behavior is often rooted in fear.

Working Moms are True Superheroes!

Before I close this chapter out, I need to say this loud and clear:

Women lawyers who are moms are true superheroes.

I say this all the time to the dear friends of mine who practice law and raise their children: All that you do is amazing!

Child-rearing is exhausting. Right. *I get that.* But it's especially exhausting to the young lawyer who's just starting out, and to the mom who's trying to be a good parent and a good lawyer at the same time.

I want young lawyers who are parents to be willing to do the hard work of balancing family and lawyering, because it **is** a balance that can *definitely* be achieved.

Listen to this: If you're working ridiculous hours, running at one hundred miles an hour at work, making sacrifices that are encroaching on the time you spend with your family, and if you're unhappy with all of that, then I want you to know that you can change it.

Stand up to the oppressive partner who wants you to work a minimum sixty-hour workweek and say, "Look, the time I spend with my kids is precious to me, so I'm not going to be able to take this brief home with me tonight."

Decide on the type of life you want to live, then live it.

When Sandi and I have our grandkids over, the house is always a swirl of activity. Constant movement. Lots of noise.

And when they *leave*? Well, that's when we plop down on the nearest two chairs, look at each other for a second or two, then readily admit, *we're not as young as we used to be.*

To the young lawyers trying to find the comfortable space between work and home (and it does exist; I promise): Keep trying. It is entirely doable.

It's also the most important thing you'll ever do in your life.

CHAPTER SEVEN
THE MISTAKES THAT LAWYERS MAKE
OR TO BE COMPLETELY HONEST: THE MISTAKES I'VE MADE THAT YOU CAN NOW AVOID!

Ruthless

I want this to be the very first word in this chapter because it's probably the most important.

At all times and in every conceivable manner, you should be ruthless about treating your *practice* as the *business* that it is. The word "ruthless" scares some. It shouldn't. I mean, "Do not make decisions based on whim or emotion."

Data only. Please.

In this chapter, I'll tick off a laundry list of some of the mistakes and missteps I've seen lawyers make over the years. Maybe by sharing them, I can help you avoid them or least help you recognize them when they're heading your way. For most lawyers just now figuring out that they need to improve their business sense, learning to simply avoid the advertising mistakes will add profit. The marketing vultures want you to spend more. In fact, their answer to every failed marketing campaign is, "You should have spent more."

There's one particular mistake we need to talk about that deserves to be at the very top of the heap, because it's a biggie.

Lawyers who adhere to the principles of Great Legal Marketing have learned to avoid this one at all costs. Why? Because it's a mistake that could put us right back onto the path towards stressful living and unhealthy habits. Here goes:

It's a mistake to stay stuck on a path that clearly makes you miserable just to remain "obedient" to the status quo.

The grim rule and mistaken assumption that too many young lawyers come out of law school with is that there is only *one path* you can choose, and the direction you take is somehow pre-ordained by the hierarchy. They have brainwashed you into believing that stepping off that path or striking out in a different direction makes you a renegade, a rebel, and unsuitable to be a lawyer.

We like renegades and rebels. They created America. Without rebels, we lawyers would still not be allowed to advertise. Remember, it is much easier to them to convince you to climb the same "ladder of success" they did than it is for them to compete with you, a renegade.

It is a mistake to remain trapped in a world that no longer exists just because "they" say, "This is the way we did it." You deserve better. It would now be *a mistake to ignore the helping hand of experience being extended to you.*

Let me break it down. Here's what I want you to internalize.

Just because I got through law school on, more or less, the "established" path doesn't mean I have to climb the "ladder of success" law school put out there for me, especially if I am expected to endure difficult clients, constant stress, and a crumbling family life, all while doing more and more pro bono and committee work.

I am free to sidestep, leapfrog, and/or walk away from this pre-ordained path right now. I could care less about the status quo because, by definition, the status quo means "average" and I am not satisfied with "average."

This is really one of the main reasons I'm writing this chapter: To bring home the point that it's not only perfectly okay, but absolutely necessary to step off the beaten path if you want to live a life of meaning and purpose.

Will there be bumps?

There *will* be bumps.

If this were easy, everyone would be good at it and everyone would do the work necessary to get through the bumps.

The path is there.

. . .

Before I launch into my list, I need to make some important points:

1. The reason I know that these are mistakes is because I've made them myself. My theory has always been that if you see somebody walking straight towards a hole in the ground and you *know* he's going to trip or stumble (or fall in completely), why not at least yell out a warning or a word of caution? In this chapter, I'm trying to guide you

around the holes. I mean, why must you fall in if there's a way to avoid it?[3]

2.   As you read through this chapter, understand that I am not casting blame, pointing fingers, or slapping you on the wrist for bad behavior. Most of these mistakes are not your fault. They are simply a product of what you have been taught.

3.   Be clear: The established bar has been setting down these traps and snares for decades. Their patterns are powerful, pervasive, and, while they may have made some sense when the legal profession was a guild, they are ridiculously out of step with the modern world. A wiser, smarter consumer, faced with more choices today than one could have ever thought imaginable just twenty years ago, demands change. You can ride that wave or keep swimming against it. Your choice.

The path set out by the establishment is acceptable only if you make the deliberate choice to be left behind. Some will, in the belief that it is safer. If you want something more out of your life and you are shown a different, better path to that result, but choose not to take it out of fear of the work involved or what others may say about you, then you have chosen to let your spouse and family down.

---

3. This reminds me of a trial I won, then lost. A lady was out walking her dog when she walked, backwards, into an uncovered "manhole." I convinced the jury to award her damages for her broken leg. The Supreme Court of Virginia upheld the trial court's decision to take the verdict away, citing Virginia's "one percent contributory negligence rule." And you thought your jurisdiction was tough!

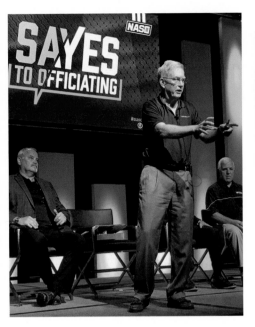

I was invited to speak at the National Association of Sports Officials conference in the summer of 2018. Here, I shared the stage with referees and umpires from the NBA, the NHL, and Major League Baseball. I told the crowd about the high school varsity soccer sportsmanship program that we had started in Northern Virginia.

I have been a soccer referee since I was 16. I continue to referee high school and youth soccer games. I love it. I turned down a chance to pursue a pro career because I valued family more.

Here is the sportsmanship banner that hangs at many fields in Northern Virginia. We give these banners out for free. Feel free to take a stand and steal this idea for your community!

Annandale Boys Club travel soccer, 1970. This was the team I joined after my dad told me to tell the coach that I played "left fullback." All of the coaches were volunteers in the early '70s, and kids today would be surprised to see the dirt and rock fields that we played on. That's me, front row, second player in from the right.

In 1976, our team, the Annandale Boys Club "Cavaliers" were National U19 champions (McGuire Cup). Every player on this team went on to play Division 1 college soccer except Gary Etherington (front row player on the right), who went directly into the pros. I am again front row, second player in from the right.

My siblings and their spouses gathered with Mom and Dad for Thanksgiving in 2018. My mother passed away several months later and over 300 people attended her funeral. She left quite a legacy.

Facing Goliath?

Hire a battle-proven attorney who can help you win.

Now there is an attorney you can trust to get justice. Benjamin W. Glass, III, has over 15 years of courtroom experience, helping clients win their battles. If you are in need of an attorney to represent you in serious cases of personal injury and medical malpractice, Ben Glass is the right choice. With a proven track record of successful litigation, Ben Glass has helped many members of our Fairfax community overcome their Goliath.

Call (703) 591-9829 for a FREE Consultation or Visit Ben's Web site at www.vamedmal.com

This "David and Goliath" ad was my first "official" ad after my solo practice was formed. I looked up "advertising agency" in the Yellow Pages and this is what I got. Never leave your marketing to the advertising companies!

WILLIAM & MARY

SOCCER 1977

Several of my Cavalier teammates and I played soccer for William and Mary. In 1977, I made the cover of the Press Guide. I also spent a lot of time refereeing around the Tidewater Peninsula. It was the best part of college because that's where I met Sandi.

Sandi and me on one of our first dates. What a ride it has been!

The playground lady and the engineer. My mom and dad, Ben and Pat Glass, in the mid-'70s. They raised seven children and, yes, we did have the best backyard in the neighborhood.

When Gary Etherington (far right) went directly from the Cavaliers to the New York Cosmos, my teammates Chris Davin (far left), Doug Dugan, and I would travel to New York to watch him play and practice. Here we are with Pele, the greatest player of his time.

This is the ad that generated the most hate mail. Apparently, lawyers didn't like it when I pointed out that all of their advertising was of no help to consumers.

If you were a personal injury attorney and you weren't nationally board-certified, didn't have a perfect "10" rating on AVVO, weren't listed in Best Lawyers in America *and* Super Lawyers, and didn't have a track record of success and a long list of happy clients, what would you say in your advertising?

Right. "We are aggressive."

www.TheTruthAboutLawyerAds.com

(Instant download!)

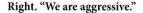

I got the idea for this ad by studying the advertising during the war between Hertz and Avis rental car companies. A knowledge of what has worked in the past is important to understanding good advertising for you.

If this were the usual personal injury law firm ad this space would be filled with a picture of a gory accident scene, a fistful of dollars, a gavel, or a meaningless platitude like "We Care."

How silly. Most attorney ads do nothing to help you find the best lawyer for your case. We are the only personal injury law firm in Virginia to offer over 400 consumer-friendly videos (**LegalAcademyVideos.com**) and the following books (electronic download or mailed to your home or office before you go for the "free" initial consultation).

Before **You Talk To The Insurance Adjuster, Hire An Attorney, or Sign Any Forms**

- Free **downloads** at www.FreeLawGuides.com
- Call 703-520-2883 to order **books** (yes, 100% free and no hassle)
- Call 703-520-2892 to speak to a *real* **attorney** *(no charge, no stress)*
- Submit your **question** *(free and confidential)* at JustAskBenGlass.com

BEN**GLASS**LAW™

FREE Books Before You Sign ANY Form

Really Cool and Slightly Outrageous
ADVERTISING MATERIAL

I got the idea for this ad from a financial services ad. We make it a habit of looking at what other successful companies are doing and then "borrowing" their ideas and importing them into our own marketing. It also drew fire from competitors.

This is the first page of an ad from Nightingale-Conant for Dan Kennedy's Magnetic Marketing product. This is the ad that changed everything for me. I took what was for me at the time a big gamble and invested $300 in the product. I knew that if I could understand what Dan Kennedy was teaching it would change my life. I now understand and teach it myself.

United States District Court

EASTERN DISTRICT OF VIRGINIA
ALEXANDRIA DIVISION

CATHERINE GROOM,	**JUDGMENT IN A CIVIL CASE**
V.	
CHARLES A. ENGH, M.D.	

CASE NUMBER: 86-0293-A

☒ **Jury Verdict.** This action came before the Court for a trial by jury. The issues have been tried and the jury has rendered its verdict.

☐ **Decision by Court.** This action came to trial or hearing before the Court. The issues have been tried or heard and a decision has been rendered.

IT IS ORDERED AND ADJUDGED that the plaintiff, Catherine Groom, recover of the defendant Charles A. Engh, M.D., the sum of FIVE HUNDRED THOUSAND AND NO/100($500,000.00) Dollars, with interest thereon at the rate as provided by law, and her costs of action.

Not yet three years out of law school, I won my first medical malpractice case against a world-famous hip surgeon. This was the judgment order.

Again, acceptable if by deliberate choice. I'd at least give them a say in your decision.

Ponder that.

. . .

Okay, so I should also mention that there's a boatload of other mistakes that won't be included on this list, but those might be for another book.

If you're making any of these mistakes right now in your life or in your practice, stop.

And if you haven't made them yet, don't start.

It's a Mistake to Believe That the Skills that Make You a Good Lawyer Will Suffice to Help You Create a Great Law Firm

I'm going to keep hammering this point home until it feels like your new mantra.

Separating the practice of law from the business of law is a MUST—and for most lawyers the "business-building" part is an acquired skill. If it really felt natural to us we would have been business majors who stayed in school a few more years to get our MBAs.

We went to law school to learn torts and contracts and what happens if you shoot an intruder who is within the curtilage of your house.

Who cares if you aced the bar exam? The skills that make you a good lawyer are not the same skills that allow you to run your practice as a thriving, profitable business. Today, both skills are necessary.

I know, I know. This is not what you learned in law school. All you ever heard in law school and from the established bar is that,

"If you do good work they will come." Total B.S.

If you're treating your practice as just a practice, the overwhelming probability is that you will blend right in with the hundreds of other lawyers in your community. Expand your thinking and be a "forever learner." Your family is depending on you.

The Billable Hour is One of the Dumbest Ideas for the Modern Lawyer

It also happens to be anti-consumer.

You never want to limit yourself by charging by the hour. The fact of the matter is that the more experience you get under your belt, the *faster* and more efficiently you can actually solve problems. If you're fast and efficient at solving problems, then how in the world does it make sense to charge by the hour? The client has a problem to solve. There is a price (fee) that you are willing to do the work for and the client is willing to pay. This may mean that you have different fees for different clients for the same work. As long as the client is empowered to make a hiring decision based on full disclosure of what fee you will charge, it is no one else's business what that fee is. The client is, after all, free to *not* hire you.

Don't underprice yourself. If you are truly adding value to a client's life, then price your services accordingly. I am fully aware of the admonition that a lawyer's fees must be reasonable, so don't send me hate mail about that. "Reasonable" is in the eyes of the consumer and as long as it is the consumer making a rational decision (meaning, not based on force or fraud) then the consumer decides, not anyone else. Your job is to make yourself valuable. We have GLM members across the country who routinely make themselves very valuable in just about every practice area.

A fee agreement based on the billable hour, besides limiting you to the number of hours in a day, is also one of the scariest transactions a consumer will ever enter into.

"Let me get this straight. I am going to get a divorce but you have no idea how much it's going to cost me?" This is horrifying to most rational people. Figure out how to make money and be consumer friendly.

Don't stick with the billable hour just because that's the way it's always been done. Talk to other lawyers who've tried another model . . . and got it right.

Here's one:

Lee Rosen, a North Carolina lawyer with a lucrative family law practice, was one of the first to go all-in with the flat-fee model in family law matters—and he really nailed it, too. He got it *right* when others said it was impossible to do. Lee was bold enough to buck the system and create a new model, and it paid off big-time.

I interviewed Lee for my coaching members a while back. If you'd like a CD of the interview, send me your name and address and I'll send it to you for free. It's worth a listen. (This is also a special prize for reading so far and paying attention.)

Most Lawyers Are Boring. Stop Being Boring

Ask your next client who had surgery more than three years ago who their surgeon was and they probably can't tell you. Why? That person was only a "surgeon" to them and once their problem was solved, there was no reason to remember the surgeon's name. That's bad news for the surgeon, especially if he relies on referrals from patients for new business.

You limit your opportunities when you present yourself to the outside world as a lawyer and a lawyer only. People are actually

pretty scared of lawyers. I remember meeting a fellow CrossFit®
athlete at our local "box." She is a family practice doctor. Her first
reaction when hearing that I am a personal injury attorney was
mild repulsion. We have since become friends. She refers me cases
because she now knows me as the "CrossFit® Dad to Nine Who
Also Referees Soccer Games."

Our profession is way too buttoned-up and one-dimensional.
We take ourselves too seriously and thus, we bore people. Being
boring is a big, preventable mistake.

Fortunately, this mistake has an easy solution. All you have
to do is start talking to other people about something *other* than
your law practice! Share a part of yourself that *isn't* tied to your
profession.

All of us have outside interests and passions (if we're healthy
and well-balanced, that is). Making those interests known sets you
apart from others, which also happens to be the best marketing
strategy around. Make yourself more memorable.

I am more than my practice.

Okay, so I'll be the guinea pig here:

In my world, people know me far beyond just Ben Glass Law.
Sure, lots of people know that I'm a good lawyer with a couple
of thriving businesses and a kick-ass team of professionals who
help drive the engine of Ben Glass Law and Great Legal Marketing. But just as many might know me as a father with nine kids
(four adopted from China), or the guy who does CrossFit®, or the
guy who's always out there on the soccer field coaching or refereeing games.

Here's my point:

*I am more than my practice and I am not afraid of letting people
find out about those parts of my life.* Note that I said "find out." You
can be boorish if you brag about yourself. That's almost worse than

being boring. You have to find a way to tell your non-lawyer stories in a way that inspires. This is not easy.

Here's the key:

Every person has a unique story. You can't steal mine and I can't steal yours. Showing the full picture of who Ben Glass is makes me more memorable, more relatable, and more accessible. My fingerprint is unlike anyone else's in the world.

So is yours.

Opening Up

A friend of mine recently shared a story with me which really moved me deeply; it's a story he'd never shared before (not with me, anyway).

He told me his mother died when he was a very young boy. Shortly after his mom's death, his father, who was very high up in the military, stepped down from his military career so that he could raise his two young boys and be there for them whenever they needed him. *He gave up his entire, distinguished military career for his kids.*

During that same conversation, he also shared with me that that his mother's death, which was a result of medical malpractice, was what drove him to become a lawyer in the first place.

Deeply personal stuff.

I'd known this guy for quite a while but he'd never revealed this part of himself before, and it touched me deeply. It also gave me another prism through which I could look at him and get a great glimpse of his human side.

The good news is that I think he's going to be opening up about this part of his life more frequently now, which I see as a good and healthy development.

It's a mistake to have people view you as only a practicing lawyer. It limits your prospects, closes off your world, and pretty much assures that you'll continue blending in with the crowded, competitive landscape.

Let your story be known.

. . .

Don't Assume That the World Owes You Anything

This one is what I consider one of the *biggest mistakes* of all time: Believing that the market owes you something because of your hard work to build a practice, your dedication to your clients, your law degree from a famous law school,[4] and your service to the profession.

Listen up: The world owes you nothing.

The market doesn't care where you went to law school or how high you ranked in your graduating class or how much law school debt you have.

In that same vein, it's also a mistake to think that caring very deeply about your clients sets you apart from other lawyers or somehow makes you special. It doesn't.

Caring deeply about your clients doesn't automatically put you on the "good lawyer" or even the "successful lawyer" list. There are lots of poor lawyers out there who care just as deeply (or deeper) about their clients. Tooting that horn doesn't win you any extra points, nor does it generate any extra income. They *expect* you to care deeply about them.

These future clients don't belong to you. Yet, it's your job to convince them that you are the right choice over all the other choices they have (including the choice to not hire a lawyer).

So drop the entitlement mentality. Money does not move to the entitled.

---

4. While I was writing this book I visited the "land of lawyer advertising," Florida, where I found a lawyer proclaiming on his billboard ad that he is a "Harvard Law School graduate." I'm sure his mother is very proud of him.

Law Schools, Listen Up: It's A Huge Mistake To Neglect Teaching the Business of the Practice of Law

Understand that your law students need to learn about business, too. It's a mistake to not at least offer them the *option* of taking a few business classes. *Lawyers need to learn the business of lawyering.* Simple as that.

My Message (and My Offer) to Law Professors

If you're that law professor who is actually teaching your students the business of law, first off: Thank you. We need more of you out there. Second: I'd like to promise that I'll provide as many free copies of this book as you tell me you need. Just contact me. (I'd like to meet you anyway!)

The Very, Very Sad (and Frustrating) Symposium

Recently, I listened to an audio recording of a ninety-minute symposium of Virginia law school deans who were all very excited about the fact that they were expanding their roster of law classes to include "wellness" classes that focus on mental well-being, stress reduction, yoga, et cetera.

All of that is okay and rather harmless, but by itself it's just not enough, and to suggest that these law school curriculum changes are going to have a profound effect on the profession is delusional.

My question is this: How in the world can they say, "Look, we're going to teach you meditation and stress reduction classes," but not say a single word about business classes that would help their students to become self-sufficient and market-savvy when it's time to go out into the real world?

To law students: If you can't find the resources you need to learn more about the business of law, trek over to the community college and take a couple of business classes. Read a couple of books by other successful entrepreneurs to see how they did it. Instead of law review, try something that teaches you about business! In fact, if your plan is to get a part of a small law firm, then I want to congratulate you. The world needs more like you—entrepreneurial and innovative.

It's A Mistake to Think That the Client is Your Master. This Should Never, *Ever* be the Case

Let me share a story:

Sandra Day O'Connor, Retired Associate Justice of the Supreme Court of the United States, was the featured speaker at my son Brian's law school graduation.

Justice O'Connor told the graduates that as graduates soon to be lawyers, they must now, "Serve a new master."

Uh, no.

To law graduates and young lawyers I want to say this: Your role as lawyer is one of a trusted adviser and life coach, not slave. The client is no more your master any more than a patient is the master of the doctor. Your role is to prescribe to a client who respects in order that they listen to your advice.

You are the master. Nobody else.

Even when you serve your client, you are not a *servant*. Getting this right in your head and then taking actions which are consistent with this belief will make you happier.

Don't Take the Small Cases Just to Keep the Lights On

When I was a young lawyer, an older lawyer at a big TV advertising firm told me that the reason they turned no case away was that "the small case of today is the big case of tomorrow." The small cases will find you, especially when you first go out on your own: other lawyers will call, congratulate you on being so smart to start your own practice, then try to dump their dogs on you. One "established bar" mantra you will hear is that one rung of the ladder of success *is* taking other people's bad cases "for the experience." This is nonsense.

Working with bad cases and (often) bad clients that others have dumped is a recipe for misery. It's better to volunteer your time sitting second chair to an experienced trial attorney in your area. Remember: always play up!

If you are a personal injury lawyer, let the settlement mills handle those really crappy cases. (I've recently published a small consumer book that tells accident victims when they should hire a settlement mill for their case. How's that for interesting marketing?) For you, any decision that *doesn't* support and reinforce your overall business plan is a mistake and it's usually not a good idea to have "we handle crappy cases" as a part of your plan.

Now, I once had a lawyer "protest" and say to me, "But, Ben, isn't everyone entitled to justice, even if they have a smaller case?"

My response: "Not if it interferes with the goals I have set out for my life." No one is *entitled* to my labor. But here's the good news for my friend: once you have a steady case flow and you develop great systems for handling the work you have, *this* will free you to take on more marginal cases by either expanding your staff (smartly) or by developing relationships with younger lawyers to whom you can refer the cases (for a fee) *and mentor.*[5] (More on mentoring in an upcoming chapter.)

---

5. The caveat here is that you should never take on a case out of guilt. Whether it's *pro bono* work or a crappy case, take it only if it advances your life. Taking on cases because they are interesting or challenging advances your life. Taking on a case simply to meet a *pro bono* quota will only add to your misery.

See? My solutions are win-win-win.

Here's what I suggest: Rather than taking on the small cases that you *know* are going to cost you more in your time than you're *ever* going to get back, why not use that time to sit down and read a good business book or listen to a good podcast on entrepreneurship? Over the long run, investing in this kind of professional development is a far better use of your time.

I know, I know. This is very difficult advice to swallow when you have a low or unpredictable cash flow. I get that. But the dangerous cycle you're creating (and perpetuating) is the potential for you to stay stuck in this pattern. I have seen it over and over again. As Bruce Springsteen sings, "It's a death trap . . . and we've got to get out while we can."

Look at your own entrepreneurial development as an even more important investment than law school. Law school, like your gym membership, gets you in the door, but there's a lot more work to be done, which is best done if directed by a trainer if you really want to get the most out of your membership.

It's a mistake to stay stuck in the "small-cases" trap. Be brave enough to stand up and say, "Enough!" to the small cases.

Bad Clients Don't Deserve You

Keeping bad clients is disrespectful to your team.

I have zero tolerance for clients who act disrespectfully or cause undue stress to me and/or my team. I defend my team. You should, too.

If I'm talking to a bad client on the phone, I try to keep my door open so that my team can hear how I'm handling the situation, which is usually by saying, "Hey, I'm giving you a chance here, but let me tell you what you're *not* going to do moving forward. You're *not* going to keep making unreasonable demands or cause stress and aggravation to me or my team. It you can't accept that, then I can gladly help you find another lawyer."

Sucking up to sucky clients is a mistake.

Keeping on a bad client will burn out your staff—and in most cases, it will be your staff who's going to be dealing with the knuckleheads the majority of the time, anyway. *Your staff is your most important asset.*

If it comes down to a choice between a crappy client and a solid member of my team, I can promise you this: *The staff will always, always win out.*

It's *difficult* to turn a client away or send a client packing because, after all, they did come to you because of some perceived need. And since you've always been trained to believe that you have no choice in the matter, it doesn't feel right to fire a client.

Well, it's wrong *not* to do it if that client is causing you frustration, stress or discord amongst your team members.

One small caveat about crappy clients:

It's important to always keep in mind that while some are just assholes, the difficult client is sometimes *being* difficult because of the stress of whatever it is that caused him to seek you out in the first place.

There is a place for grace. We start with seeking to understand, but when that client crosses the line from reacting to fear to being an outright jerk to your or your staff, it's time to take action. Fire him.

Another side note: *Many years ago, I remember taking on a client (an asshole, it turned out) who'd been referred to me by another client. I really wanted to get rid of that new client, but* *the plain and simple truth was that as a young lawyer I was worried about disappointing the referral source.*

I made the mistake of keeping on a bad client out of fear of disappointing the referring client. At the end, no one was happy.

Let me repeat: Making fear-based decisions is *always* a bad mistake.

Don't Stay on the Court-Appointed List for Too Long

Here's another story: I met a young lawyer in my community who was a couple of years into his practice and, for the most part, already completely burned out. He and his wife were "ships passing in the night."

He was a good criminal defense attorney who took his responsibility very seriously—but most of his cases were appointed by the court, which meant, in Virginia, he was working for below minimum wage. (Which I thought was illegal! "Fifteen dollars per hour for everyone except licensed attorneys representing the indigent!")

Because he was relatively new to the practice of law, he didn't feel as though he was in a strong enough position to stand up to the judges in his small county and say, "Look. I'm happy to help out with some cases but can't take all of the ones you send me." In this particular jurisdiction the judges insisted that its court-appointed lawyers take "all or nothing," thus enslaving the lawyer. Sad that a highly trained and deeply indebted lawyer did not feel he was able to stand up to "authority." Another good person likely soon headed out of the profession.

Here's the deal: The court-appointed list is a great way for young lawyers to get early experience, but this, too, is a great example of being sucked into the vortex if you allow yourself to stay on that underpaid and overworked list for so long that it prevents you from building a life for yourself.

I *get that* it's difficult to stand up to judges. I used to think they were god-like too. (Now I see those I "grew up in the law" with on the bench. Many good folks, some real jerks, but no deities, far as I can tell.) Until you start bucking the status quo, until you start rejecting industry norms, things will not change.

. . .

The most important thing to remember in the midst of all of these mistakes is this:

We can fix this.

These mistakes can be avoided moving forward. No, they cannot be erased from the past, but they can be seen as lessons that you will never, ever forget.

And remember this: Making some mistakes is an important part of creating the kind of life you want to live. Building your perfect life doesn't happen overnight, and the process is not perfect. Mistakes are where lessons are taught.

Making a mistake doesn't mean you're a failure. Pick yourself up, brush yourself off, and keep on walking. Just make sure that you don't keep doing the same thing over and over and thinking that things will turn out differently tomorrow. The change you want begins with you.

It's never too late to change.

CHAPTER EIGHT
ADVERTISING MISTAKES TO AVOID

"Advertising"

What does that word even mean? Let me give you a couple of definitions that are useful to know and understand before we start:

- "Advertising" is a message delivered via a medium that is designed to attract the attention of someone who isn't already aware of you.

- "Brand advertising" is advertising that does little more than "get your name out there." It is virtually useless to us. How do you know if your advertising is "brand advertising?" Easy. Brand-building ads consist of little more than name; slogan; photo of you, a courthouse, or the American flag; and weak or no call to action. ("Free consultation" is weak.) There is usually only one means of responding (i.e. "call now"). Tracking your ad spend with brand advertising is virtually impossible, thus the marketing vultures love to sell it to you.

- "Direct response advertising" is advertising that provokes a response right now, and typically offers multiple ways and multiple reasons to initiate contact. Direct response advertising is usually also designed to help improve the consumer's life right now. With direct response advertising, you can accurately measure your return on investment. Direct response advertising allows you to send targeted advertising that is specific to the prospect, via a well-designed follow up system. Marketing vultures hate direct response advertising because it holds them accountable.

What I'm about to say next is something you already know: The fight to be noticed is fierce. You are viewed by a highly skeptical public as a commodity. You are not trusted. There are lots of "you" out there and consumers believe that they often don't actually need you to solve their problems.

The non-lawyer tech companies like Avvo™ and LegalZoom™ have much more money than you do because they can get it (and business-building expertise) from venture capitalists, while the bar *requires* you to be self-funded and does not allow you to partner up with non-lawyer business experts. The consumer can "visit," via websites, YouTube, and instant chat, a dozen law firms in an hour. Then they can hop on over to the lawyer review sites to see whether you match up to your competition.

The prospect of cutting through all that clutter is daunting, costly, and maybe even a little scary. But here's the good news: You can do it. Thousands of GLM members and followers do it every day. Solo and small firm lawyers who are not spending an arm and a leg keep up with the 800-pound gorilla you see on every TV channel, billboard, and bus. Doing well. Getting good cases. Having fun.

More good news: Since most lawyer advertising is pretty crappy and unimaginative, you really only need to be just a little better than your local competition to stand out. To the extent your competition is "learning" about marketing it is coming either from 1) other lawyers via generic "marketing" CLE courses or 2) marketing vultures, neither one of whom 1) know as much about marketing as I do and 2) are backed by thousands of lawyers just like you who are willing to share because they know that a rising tide lifts all boats.

Every month in the *Great Legal Marketing Journal* we showcase members across the spectrum of legal services who are building practices that work. Our members take what they see in the journal, improve upon it, and share their improvement with our membership. That's how we play.

Know any other lawyer groups like that?

Nope, neither do I.

Oh, and one more thing: a marketing vulture will never tell you to "stop spending your money" until you have the systems in place that can deal with the leads you will generate. I will.

If you do only one thing after reading this book, do this: insist that your marketing dollars get tracked to actual revenue. It's not a perfect science but most do nothing to track. They are either unimaginably rich or they are fools.

. . .

Okay, let's get started with the simple mistakes lawyers make. I'll go into the details later.

Let's start with a quick list, then we'll break it down:

- We don't think very deeply about legal advertising.

- We spend money on advertising (most of it going directly to the marketing vultures) without having developed a real plan for how to make sure that that money is coming back in, carrying with it a return on our investment.

- We think that because we're lawyers we're "different" than other industries and therefore *above* having to sell our services and advertise our presence.

- Most important, we haven't taken the time or made the concerted effort to dig down deep and make a decision about the kind of lives we want to be leading; we haven't paused long enough to find our "why." (And yes, this is directly related to advertising and marketing because our "why" should be what guides every single advertising decision we make.)

That last sentence stands at the heart of what GLM is all about. Every day I see lawyers ask a version of this question on a lawyer listserv: "What do you think about XYZ vendor? Because the one I have now is not producing for me."

Wrong question. I've grown tired of responding, "What's the goal? Who are you trying to attract? What kind of lifestyle do you want?" because very few ever have a good, well-thought-out theory of their business.

Spending any money on "advertising" before you answer those questions is a fool's game. It is wasteful. It's what leads to misery, stress, and frustration. It's a big part of what the National Task Force on Lawyer Wellness missed.

> **Copy This—Blow it Up—And Paste it to Your Wall**
>
> If you haven't decided what you want for your life, and if
> you haven't made the commitment to get out there and
> make it happen, there will be no focus to your marketing
> and no good reason for your advertising. Your advertis-
> ing *strategy* will be a ship without a rudder—so you might
> as well just burn your marketing dollars in a big bonfire.
> That would at least be interesting.

Again, many of the points I tick off here are based on the
principles of Great Legal Marketing, with one big difference: most
GLM lawyers are avoiding these mistakes. This is why they are
completely comfortable with coming up against—or should I say
moving away from—the status quo and towards a life of meaning
and purpose. GLM lawyers have already chosen a different path.

Just as I said in the earlier chapter, I share these mistakes with
you in hopes you'll learn from them and maybe avoid them when
they come your way.

Mistake #1:
Being Shy About Marketing in the First Place

You may have picked up this book because you are curious but
not yet convinced that aggressively marketing yourself and your
practice is the "right" thing to do. You may even be afraid of what
your fellow lawyers might think about you.

Let me help you get over those feelings.

In my large home office in Fairfax Station, Virginia, my wife,
Sandi, has decorated my wall with this sign: *You are a Child of
God, Your Playing Small Does Not Serve the World*. Ponder this for a
moment: If you're a good lawyer and right now there is someone

in your community with a legal issue and you would be the best lawyer for them, why in the world would you let that person wander aimlessly into the office of a lawyer who would not be perfect for that person?

If you are the right person, then it is your moral duty to make yourself known to them and get them into your office. In order to do this, your marketing must be really good and it must be backed by a belief that yes, you are the right person for some.

Play big. You have a unique set of gifts and talents. Why let them lay dormant with "shy" marketing?

Mistake #2:

Looking Around at What All the Other Lawyers Are Doing and Saying "I Want Some of That, Too"

A popular marketing vulture line is to tell you that "Lawyer XX down the street is buying lots of ads on my platform, wouldn't you like some, too?" Since you have no idea what Lawyer XX's ROI is or whether Lawyer XX is anything more than a marketing victim himself, "following" XX to the cashier is idiotic. The idiocy is often compounded by the fact that you don't have systems and people in place to properly follow up on and handle the leads that just might be generated from the marketing vulture's platform.

Think like a business owner and go looking outside the legal industry for ideas. At Ben Glass Law, I saw that most personal injury lawyer advertising was designed to reach people who had already decided that hiring a lawyer was the right thing to do. The ads all have the same messages, "We are aggressive," or "No fee if no recovery," and "We care for you." At the same time we knew that following an accident, three things were happing to accident victims:

1. They were getting called by insurance adjusters.

2. They were filling out forms at their doctor's offices.

3. While they might be thinking about hiring a lawyer, they had no experience in that process.

Our own experience with clients told us that for most, "getting the most money they deserved" was *not* what they were looking for when they hired an attorney. No, they wanted to make sure that they would not be financially ruined if they had medical bills to pay and they could not work.

Not seeing any lawyer adverting that seemed to make sense to me, I looked outside the legal industry for answers. When I looked I found:

1. A real estate agent in Canada who offered free information reports to prospective sellers of houses that provided tips on preparing to put a house up for sale.

2. A carpet cleaning company that offered a "consumer guide to choosing the right carpet cleaner for your house."

3. A financial services broker who had actually written a book that taught people how to invest "on your own."

I played prospect and requested their marketing material because I had heard, in my hanging out with non-lawyer entrepreneurs, that all of these people were wildly successful in their industries. I discovered what all of these successful people had in common: They were writing information pieces and providing it free to prospects as a way of 1) getting consumers to identify themselves to the businesses and 2) establishing themselves as authorities in their fields.

Once I started producing books, CDs and DVDs that provided free information to car accident victims, everything changed. Our marketing message went from "free consultation" to "If you have been in an accident you may not need a lawyer, but before you talk to the adjuster, sign any forms, or hire an attorney, get our free book."

Had I simply said, "I want more of what lawyers are doing to advertise," my practice would have remained average. Failing to actively cultivate an entrepreneurial mindset is a big mistake.

Mistake #3:
Underestimating the Challenge

Some lawyers brush off the challenge presented by the non-lawyer tech companies by thinking, "Well, it would be pretty dumb for a consumer to think that they are going to get really good legal service from those companies, I've seen them mess up a lot of wills and stuff."

At a recent bar-sponsored event I attended in Virginia, the speaker joked about and demeaned Avvo™. The crowd of over 200 laughed right along with the speaker. Big mistake! First, the one thing most of these companies excel at is service. They figured out that most consumers believe (because it happens to be true) that dealing with lawyers is an expensive hassle. The tech companies were quick to figure out how to build a better experience for the consumer.

Lots of money plus lots of business expertise equals happier consumers.

Coupled with that idea is this: we forget just how very scary it is for a consumer to interact with us. We think we are friendly, but they have likely never had to interact with a lawyer before. Moreover, all they've heard about is that we are assholes.

I said it earlier but it is worth a reminder: consumers have lots of choices, including the choice to not do anything about their problem. You can't do what all of the other lawyers are doing and hope to stand out.

Mistake #4:
Panicking and Falling for the "Deal of the Week"

I'll be the first to admit it: I've spent a lot of what I call "dumb money" on advertising mistakes. Looking back, it makes me realize how naïve I was when I first started out; how impressionable. But that's where I was in my life at the time, desperate for cases and cash flow and not knowing that there was a better way.

Well, if I hadn't been there then, I wouldn't be here now. So I count it all as an education—an *expensive* education, but an education nonetheless.

Here are a couple of examples:

The Union Magazine

This encounter occurred very early in my career, but I still remember it clearly: A guy called me one day and asked if I was interested in being *the lawyer* in the "union directory". He explained that my name will be used exclusively, and that—here's the good part—they distribute about 40,000 of these directories to their union members.

Well, of course I thought I'd really hit the jackpot, even though I was so inexperienced I'm not all that sure I even knew what the "jackpot" *was*.

So this young, naïve lawyer named Ben Glass, ready and raring to get out there and make his mark in the world of advertising, said, "Okay, let's do it! That sounds awesome!"

Big mistake.

He'd reeled me in, hook, line, and sinker. And what did I know? I was *happy* to be his catch of the day.

So I sent him my money (another big mistake). I think it was about four or five thousand dollars, which was a lot of money back then, especially since I didn't have very much of it.

Needless to say, it turned out to be a pure, 100 percent **scam.** The guy wasn't even a union representative. And there was no manual, of course. It didn't exist.

It's kind of amusing, now, to look back on the experience and remember how much I *didn't* know.

Ask me whether I thought it was funny at the time it happened.

The Goliath Ad

Very early into my solo practice, I was offered the chance to buy an ad in a local soccer tournament program, which I was more than happy to do, but I was new to the game of advertising. I didn't have a "camera-ready ad." I didn't have a graphic designer. I didn't know where to turn. I just needed an ad!

So this is what I did: I went straight to Yellow Pages and flipped to "A" for "advertising firms." Seriously. This is what I did!

Back then, the Yellow Pages was *it*. It held all the answers, and everybody looked to it as the gold standard in advertising, especially small businesses.

This was the deal: I had no clue what I was doing. The only thing I really had was the desire to get my name out there and the entrepreneurial instinct to know that I needed to hire someone to help me do it. (Okay, so I might not have known what the hell I was doing, but I still give myself an A for effort.)

As a result of my super-sophisticated search through the Yellow Pages, I ended up hiring an advertising firm that had a solid, traditional reputation. They knew the business, I'd told them what I wanted, and they got right to work. (And, they were listed under "advertising" in the Yellow Pages.)

When it was time to show me what they'd come up with, the staging and presentation of the ad took on a very dramatic flair. I remember they invited me to their local office, took me into the boardroom where the ad itself was positioned on top of a huge, gleaming conference table. Of course they kept the ad completely concealed until the moment of what I now call the big reveal.

Very dramatic stuff, indeed. It felt like I was in Hollywood, on the set of *Mad Men*—or at least in Las Vegas, watching David Copperfield or some other famous magician pull a rabbit out of a hat.

Since this was the first ad I've ever had "professionally done" by an advertising company, I just thought the whole thing was *awesome*! I do want to point out that while I was satisfied with the final product, I'd *still* been sucked in, not only by the allure and sophistication of having an ad designed by professionals, but by the dramatic flourish of the big reveal.

The headline of the ad was, "Facing Goliath," and the subtitle was, "Hire a Battle Proven Attorney who can help you Win."

The ad itself, of course, made just about every mistake an ad could make. It urged readers to "call for a free consultation," and was about as generic and boilerplate as an ad could get.

But it was *my* ad, it looked cool, and I was proud of it.

My mistake wasn't in hiring the ad firm, but in hiring an ad firm thinking that I could turn over the marketing to someone else. You can delegate the execution of the marketing, but you can't delegate the thinking about the marketing.

This is your job!

Don't leave it to the marketing vultures to teach you, because they won't. Jump in and learn as much as you can on your own.

In fact, marketing is really the business that you are in.

Here's how we can loop this experience back to the challenges we face in today's competitive world:

Today, the big reveal isn't with print ads. Today, advertising and marketing firms are revealing new websites. And when that URL goes live and lawyers see their pictures and names emblazoned across the screen, they're blown away.

Just like I was.

If your web designer "unveils" a website where the top half of the main page shows you, your office, your cityscape, or the American flag, *fire them*. They are vultures who don't understand effective marketing and they are stealing your family's money.

The Yellow Pages

This one wasn't so much a bad mistake as it was a good lesson. I use this Yellow Pages example to remind me of how far I've really come.

Shortly after I started my own firm, it came time for my Yellow Page renewal. I still remember it clearly: I didn't have a lot of money, but yet I knew I had to have an image or some sort of eye-catching ad in the Yellow Pages. (I knew I couldn't *not* have a presence.) So I created one.

I worked so hard on that ad. I gave it quite a bit of thought and eventually came up with this dollar-bill-size ad that said, "We Care for You."

It was for me, at the time anyway, a major advertising decision, and I can still remember very clearly how *cool* I thought that ad was going to look!

Today when I refer to that experience in my seminars and talks, I call it, "My personal contribution to the Yellow Pages."

Oh, how the world has changed.

Be Careful with Buying Third-Party Generated Leads

A big mistake that lots of lawyers make when they don't know what else to do is to go out and purchase leads from third-party vendors. Be careful with this one: The marketing vultures are very good about smelling your desperation.

Here's a typical pitch: "Hey, Ben, we want you to be the exclusive personal injury lawyer in our directory for Fairfax, Virginia! This will bring in more prospects than ever!"

Lawyers who are desperate will say, "Great! That sounds wonderful! Let's do it!" The guys and gals on the other end of the phone can sound very compelling, all bragging about their "proprietary systems using artificial intelligence."

Lawyers who succumb to the temptation to buy leads from any of the lead generator marketing vultures without spending any time or money actually thinking about how they can do this on their own or without having in place a system for tracking and following up on the leads are putting the cart before the horse.

Stop the bad spend first.

It's tempting when you don't have your own good lead flow—but third-party lead generators are almost always a mistake. As part of the program here at GLM, we've tested a number of them with Ben Glass Law. The consumers who are filling out a form at a "we have the best lawyers" generic lead generation site have likely already filled out forms, and been rejected, by real lawyers.

If you have fallen for this tactic before, don't worry, you are in good company. In fact, I recently had State Farm sales agents in the training center at my office. I was teaching them how to improve their businesses and sell more insurance. I asked what they spent their marketing budget on and they told me, "Third-party car insurance lead generation sites." When I asked how that was going for them they replied, in unison, "It sucks, but we don't know what else to do."

> At every moment and at every stage of the advertising process, you *have* to know how your money is moving: how much is going out, and how much is coming in. Sure, this requires time and effort, but this isn't something you can leave to the marketing vultures because they will lie about it.
>
> And here, I'll say it again: The marketing vultures don't *want* you to keep track of your own leads! Why would they? Their only purpose is to sell, sell, sell. It's not in their best interest to teach you how to follow up, track, or monitor because for most, if you knew how to track you'd be mad at them.

Mistake #5:

Inadequate Follow-Up

Don't you dare give up too soon!

Another *major* mistake is to assume that if the lead doesn't sign with you on that very day, you probably lost that lead altogether. Because they give up on leads too early and never tried smart follow-up marketing, most lawyers think that an unconverted lead has just moved on to the next lawyer on their list.

Wrong, wrong, wrong.

Our experience at Ben Glass Law is that most personal injury clients don't even *think about* signing a contract until anywhere from four to twelve months after they've become a lead for us! We know this because we track leads carefully and we can determine when they first became aware of us and when they signed a fee contract. We know how many electronic and direct mail pieces they received during that time and we are continually making changes to our marketing in response to the data we are getting. The data tells us that for many seriously injured people, there is no rush to hire an attorney.

Why do they take so long? Our experience tells us that anybody who's sustained a serious injury has about 50,000 more important things to deal with in those first months than search for, investigate, and hire an attorney. We've proven over and over that those who are dealing with serious injuries aren't really thinking about hiring a lawyer immediately. *Give it time.* It's a mistake to give up too soon.[6]

Mistake #6:

Stop Talking About Yourself in Your Marketing

Right now, go check out a handful of lawyer websites and YouTube videos uploaded by lawyers. Here's what they say:

> *My name is [insert]. I've been practicing law for [XX] years. I am passionate about what I do. I treat each client individually. I went to [insert name] law school and I'm a member of [alphabet soup] organization. My practice is totally dedicated to representing [type of specialty clients.] We are aggressive.*

Is any of that memorable? Special? Something a client or prospect would brag to their friends and family about?

Nope.

---

6. And it's not just the serious cases. We recently had our associate call three months of unconverted soft tissue leads. These were cases that were not ready to sign up with us when we first spoke to them but they had all been receiving our print newsletter in the interim. We found over $50,000 in fees in those calls! Turns out that many were not running off to hire another lawyer during that time.

People who are looking for a lawyer have a problem to solve and that problem is not solved by knowing how much you "care" or where you went to law school. Get over yourself and put yourself into the shoes of your prospect who is trying to make a great decision for themselves and their family.

They will get to know you and yes, some of your biographical information may make a difference but what they want to know first is:

Can I trust you?

The problem is that what you say about yourself carries no weight.

I Don't Regret the Mistakes I Made. I'll Just Never Repeat Them.

Over the years, I've spent hundreds of thousands of dollars educating myself about advertising and marketing. Some of it was money well spent; some of it was what I've already referred to as "spending dumb money."

I don't beat myself up about the "dumb money" I've spent because I consider all of it an important part of my overall education.

The only way I'll regret my past mistakes is if I repeat them, which is very unlikely because I'm a quick learner, especially after I've been burned.

I consider it a blessing to be able to share some of these mistakes with you, simply because it might help you avoid some of them.

Which, now that I think about it, also means that I consider it a blessing that these mistakes occurred in the first place.

You'll see that some of the material in this upcoming chapter might also relate to the subject of advertising.

So let's jump right in.

Let's get into the business of marketing.

CHAPTER NINE
A MAMMOTH MARKETING PLAN

I already know how most lawyers would answer this question I'm about to ask, but that doesn't stop me from asking them. Plus, your answers will help me make my point.

These are questions about your practice, so listen up.

And answer truthfully, please. No B.S.

Ready?

What do you stand for?

If you can answer this question boldly and without the slightest hesitation, then my hat is off to you. Trouble is, most lawyers can't. They usually default to:

"I stand for justice!"

And of course there's, "I stand for the little guy!"

Or the most noble of them all? "I stand for serving the underserved!" Blah.

These are the lawyers who are focused solely on the practice of law and not the business of law. The followers. The ones who still believe that law is an avocation, a service, and a higher calling.

Wrong, wrong, wrong.

If you defaulted to any of those sappy answers I listed above (or any similar variation), don't beat yourself up about it. It's not your fault. Just listen to what I'm going to say next, because it's important.

If you want to guarantee the success and continued growth of your practice, these three things are absolutely essential:

1. Having a set of core principles and beliefs that stand at the very center of your practice.

2. Being able to articulate those beliefs boldly, passionately, and without the slightest hesitation.

3. Being ready to stand up for those beliefs at any time and at all times.

Here's the problem, though, and it's a running theme throughout this book: the established bar limits passion. Bold statements of belief are a definite *no-no*, especially if those beliefs run along the lines of "yes, for some prospective clients, I am the best choice they could make." Self-appointment as "wise man at the top of the mountain" is, well, *against the rules*.

I once had a lawyer "call me out" on a listserv, whining that I should not be able to name my *marketing* company "*Great* Legal Marketing" because lawyers can't say they are "great." She threatened to "report" me. I had to point out to her that the prohibition against self-aggrandizement only applied to what I say about myself in the law, not in marketing, refereeing, or CrossFit®, all of which I'm pretty good at, especially for an old guy.

I'll be the first to admit that I used to be one of those lawyers. I was sucked in by the status quo and held hostage there for almost twenty years—until I discovered there was a better way to live. And, since this is a book about marketing and not technically, an "advertisement" for legal services, let me make it clear: at Ben Glass Law, we are great at what we do. We aren't for everyone, but those who we accept into "the family" as clients get a combination of great legal service and top-of-the-line customer service. And, like we tell our prospective clients, you can check us out yourself at JustReadTheReviews.com.

You've heard the saying, *you don't know what you don't know,* right? Well, I didn't know—not until the very moment that I knew—this one, simple fact: There are no rules. And there certainly aren't any rules that say that a lawyer cannot have a great life *and* be a great lawyer. In fact, having a great life and a balanced existence leads to being a *better* lawyer. The two things kind of go hand in hand.

Whenever you hear someone pronounce a "rule" of the profession, ask yourself, "Who made that rule?" For example, many lawyers believe that you have to wait to the end of a case to get a client to leave an online review for you. Ask yourself: "Who made that rule?" (Answer: there is no such rule.)

But you've got to have a core set of beliefs to get you there.

Before I go any further with this theme (and I promise to loop back to it because it's what this chapter is all about), I want to side-track for a second.

Even though I went into the details of how I was led to Magnetic Marketing® in an earlier chapter, I want to give a quick thumb-nail again because if it hadn't been for that journey, you wouldn't be holding this book in your hands right now—and you definitely wouldn't be reading this chapter about a "mammoth marketing plan."

I discovered Magnetic Marketing® shortly after I'd left my old firm. Having practiced law for over a decade by then, I was fairly confident about the stuff I knew; put simply, I was confident that I knew enough about the practice of law.

But I was becoming more and more aware that there was stuff that I didn't know about the *business* of law, and I wanted to find out.

So I started searching out resources and seeking out "success literature" that could teach me more. I became a customer of Nightingale-Conant, which at the time was a primary source for business, success and motivational tapes, and literature.

They steered me in the right direction, alright.

In fact, they sent me a letter that guided me straight towards Dan Kennedy's Magnetic Marketing® plan. (Thank you, Nightingale-Conant!)

That single letter changed the trajectory of my entire life. Some say I was "lucky" but successful people make their own luck. Lots of people got those Nightingale-Conant catalogs. I bought stuff, then I actually listened to the tapes when they arrived.

The more I read and learned about Magnetic Marketing® the more intrigued I became. What interested me most, though, was the prospect of trying to figure out a way to apply the general prin-ciples of the program to the specific practice of law.

From that point forward, my belief system began to change. My priorities began to shift. My practice and my life opened up in ways I never could have imagined when I figured out that marketing was job number one.

Ask me *what changed,* exactly, and my answer would be this: *Everything.*

But the most important shift of all? My mindset. I could go to a lot of CLEs and become a marginally better lawyer. I could figure out how to market the practice and leapfrog over most of the competition. Giving myself "permission" to take that shortcut was huge. It took me a long time to "get there" because there were so many voices out there saying, "Just do good work and they will come, marketing is for losers."

Remember the high school teenager I described a few chapters back who sold T-shirts and soccer stuff out of his locker? Well, that was when my entrepreneurial spirit first flickered to life.

Fast forward a few decades and that flicker comes roaring back as a flame, thanks to the discovery of Dan Kennedy, Magnetic Marketing®, and the mindset that it was okay to build my own life within the law—I didn't have to do what everyone else said I should do.

So only a few pages in, this chapter on marketing has offered up a couple of "must-haves" that are essential to the success of your practice. Here they are again:

1. You have permission to reject industry norms and say "who made that rule?" to *everything.*

2. If you would be perfect for a particular client, then it is your duty to do *everything* in your power to get that client into your office.

Both are critical to your success.

. . .

Okay, go ahead and ask me. I'm dying to tell you.

What do I stand for?

What I stand for today, as Ben Glass the individual, the lawyer, and the business owner, is living a life based upon a central principle, not whim.

Go ahead and ask me this, too.

Well, Ben, what is it?

The world owes me nothing. Where I am today is a product of the decisions I have made in the past; where I will be in the future is a product of the decisions I make starting today. Decisions to act, that is.

Note that the previous paragraph can be shortened to one word: decide.

Knowing the kind of life you want and creating the kind of business you want—these are the principles I am all about. We will talk more about "philosophy" in the next chapter but successful people start with having this clarity of mind.

This is also what will attract clients and will ultimately define your entire marketing plan. (And we all know that your marketing strategies are, beyond a doubt, your most important assets.) In a nutshell, this is the stuff that will make you magnetic.

Take a minute and re-read the statement of my personal and business principle above. Some will be repelled. "Well, what about [insert excuse here]?"

If I have repelled you—if you cannot release yourself from the heavy chains of blaming others for life's ills, I'm not your cup of tea. I'm good with that. You are not my avatar GLM member. But maybe you said, "Yes! Finally, someone who makes a lot of sense who has wrapped up in a nice neat little package what it means to actually do well—and enjoy—the work we have chosen to do."

I've either encouraged you to join our team of thinkers or you've decided maybe you don't even want to play this sport. Either way, you and I both win. I don't want someone on my team who isn't excited about what I teach and if attending one of my events isn't serving your "best life" then it is your moral obligation to yourself and your family to not get involved.

This is why I have largely stopped speaking at general lawyer events. I get invited to speak lots of times each year. It's not all that exciting to speak in front of people who aren't thrilled that I am there. I've *decided* to not do that anymore because it doesn't fit what I want for my life. At my own events, people are there because they have genuine ambition. We fuel their fire. It's exciting for them and it's exciting for me.

Your practice should be that way, too. It's a lot more fun to walk into a practice where every day you get to meet clients who tell you that they are "thrilled and honored to be able to speak to you." You get to that place in your practice by clearly identifying:

1. What type of practice excites you.

2. What type of client you want to see walking through your door to that practice.

3. What marketing will attract *that* client and repel the rest.

That's a fun practice. It's no mystery figuring out how to build that kind of practice. The mystery is why so many lawyers have built practices that generate misery.

Today we have GLM members from every consumer practice, from coast to coast, and border to border (and beyond) who are building practices that excite them and bring them joy. *This is what practicing law should be all about.*

Practicing law can be rewarding, meaningful and, yep, *even fun*. It doesn't have to be associated with stress at the office, anxiety at home, and feeling pigeonholed into running your practice on autopilot and not on principle. All that stuff is optional. You can *choose* to create a life that brings you joy.

How in the world does a simple marketing plan ensure a happier life and a more lucrative practice? *Because it's a marketing plan with a purpose well beyond "I need more cases."* And your purpose should stand at the core of everything you do.

First Things First: Get in Step with Reality

The consumer is in charge.

At all times, you should know exactly what your avatar client thinks they want and need. Start there, not with what *you* think they need. What is the conversation that actually runs through their mind when they start to look for you? Their fears? Their concerns?

Today's competitive marketplace for legal services is dramatically different than it was a few years ago. While the established bar foolishly spends time and money protecting "our" turf with restrictions on 1) who can help people with legal needs and 2) who can own law firms, consumers are changing the way they "buy" legal services. Technology, trends, consumer preference, all of this stuff changes at break-neck speed. **The consumer of today is definitely not the consumer of yesterday.** They have a vast array of choices when it comes to legal. The established bar is actually making it much harder for lawyers to keep up with what consumers want.

Today's consumers want one simple thing: To get their problems solved. And if they can find somebody to help them solve those, they don't really care whether you have a law license or not. Remember, most consumers think that we are a pain in the ass to deal with. It doesn't help when we lawyers get caught narrowing consumer choices, as just about every state did as they shut down Avvo™'s bold attempt to bridge the legal services gap with Avvo™ Advisor®, which was an "attorney client matching service" that consumers found useful. When the Virginia Supreme Court adopted Legal Ethics Opinion 1885, it removed a choice that consumers had in buying legal services. It took away the power to decide from consumers. It violated one of my essential principles that only *you* get to decide what is right for your life.[7]

Non-lawyer entities like LegalZoom™ and Avvo™ (new ones spring up every day) are fully aware of this change in consumer preference, and they see opportunity. At this very minute, they're doing everything they can think of, as any rational business should, to create better value for consumers than lawyers do. Rather than whining about competition or building up protectionist barriers lawyers should be asking themselves, "How have we failed the consumer so badly that he is turning to online services for answers *and* how can we fix the problem ourselves by creating even greater value?"

Just as I used the word *ruthless* in an earlier chapter, the same word applies here: These non-lawyer entities are being *ruthless* in their pursuit of the consumer in search of legal service. Suddenly, we are not the only game in town, which leads me to my next point.

---

7. As far as I can tell none of the state bars that issued "anti-Avvo™" opinions asked a single consumer how they would like to buy legal services. Thus, these opinions cured a problem that did not exist, at least in the minds of consumers. Self-regulation that is nothing more than "turf protection" never works out well in the end, ask the North Carolina Dental Board and taxi drivers everywhere.

But Wait, There's More . . .

When a consumer is evaluating his interaction with you, you are no longer being compared solely with other lawyers. It's not just LegalZoom™ and all the "law companies," he's comparing you to all of the other businesses that he interacted with last week or last month or just an hour ago who have given him superior service.

The day before he reached out to your firm, chances are good that he received high-end service from his bank teller, or maybe his insurance broker. He might have ordered a sweater on Amazon and received it on his doorstep the very next day. He tracked the package that was mailed to him through virtually every stop on the journey. He didn't have to call and ask, "What's going on with my delivery?" If he ate at a franchised restaurant he got more or less a predictable experience.

Then he called your firm and the phone was answered, "Law offices." Whoever answered the phone sounded like she was being interrupted. He was spoken to using lawyer talk. Your intake team expressed no empathy for his situation. He wasn't told exactly what was going to happen next and if there was follow up, it was not immediate and helpful.

And we wonder why LegalZoom™ is killing it?

Marketing Evangelism 101: **What I Told the Pastors**

In February 2019, I invited fifty local pastors and church leaders to my GLM training center in Fairfax, Virginia, to give them a "refresher course" on what I'd call, mostly tongue-in-cheek, *Marketing Evangelism 101.*

But the fact of the matter is that even pastors must have a message that attracts new members and expands their audience, right?

The fact that they were pastors *and not lawyers* only underscores the fact that GLM principles can be successfully and easily applied to *any* business or discipline. Why? Because the principles themselves are universal. Remember that these are not just principles but *beliefs* that spring from a very practical, holistic and, yep, a very reasoned and rational approach to life and living.

Here's what I told them:

In the sales and marketing of *any* business—and yes, I told them that they were in the "business" of religion, which excited some and caused acid reflux in others—the clearer you are about the people you want to attract, the more successful you will become at magnetically attracting these people.

This is what makes Magnetic Marketing® a mammoth marketing plan.

Even though some of the pastors found this part as hard to stomach as most lawyers do, they listened all the same. This is what I said: "You must decide who your church is for. You must decide who you want to attract. Then customize a message that will attract them." Sure, most pastors will automatically default to, "Well, we want to attract everyone! Everyone is welcome!" and while this is kind and compassionate, we all know that kindness and compassion alone aren't really what's going to help you expand your audience.

In order for these pastors to grow their bases and expand their congregations, they must decide who their churches are for. That certainly doesn't mean everyone who walks through the doors is not welcome; it only means that they don't—and they shouldn't—have to try to attract everyone.

Side note: *This parallels directly with the marketing principle that your advertising doesn't have to reach everybody—it only needs to reach the audience you've identified as desirable.*

Here's what else I told them: You may think you have the greatest story that's ever been told—I mean, the message of salvation is about as great as it gets, right?—but every church and almost every religion in the world has some version of that same message, so it's actually not all that special.

I don't think anyone had ever put it quite that way to them before! I know what you are thinking: "We can take the 'repel them' stuff a little too far. You'll never get invited back." Several weeks later I was invited by some who were present to speak to another gathering to be held several months later.

If you want your congregation to grow, *differentiation will be required*. Being for everyone is terrific is you want to be average (the very definition of "everyone"). Even the local church needs to *decide* why it deserves a place in the local market. This means a sermon that's a little different, a message that's a little different—and different than the pastor down the street who's trying to attract the same parishioner. People should be able to repeat and pass on what it is you stand for, whether you are a pastor or a lawyer.

As a sidebar, I also recommended to the pastors the same book that I recommend to every lawyer I speak to: Rick Warren's *The Purpose Driven Church*. If this book isn't on your bookshelf either at home or in your office law library (or, ideally, in both), get out and buy it as soon as you can. Pay particular attention to the chapter where he describes "Saddleback Sam."

Attract Your Client Before They Need You *and* After They Need You!

Anyone who's heard me speak before or has read anything that I've written has heard me make this point before: Don't limit your marketing and advertising to clients who are just looking for a lawyer *now*.

In these crazily competitive times, marketing only "for the now" just isn't going to cut it.

> *To capture that client before and after they need you is crucial. What this means is that you've got to figure out a way to get into their lives, onto their radar, and in front of them as often as you can—not just when something bad happens.*

At Ben Glass Law, we have thousands of people on our print newsletter lists *who've never engaged us to be their lawyer. Yet.*

These are the people who've sought information from us in the past, or maybe have heard me speak at a public seminar. These are the potential clients who might have met me on the soccer field while I was refereeing their son's game or who might know me from CrossFit® or a training seminar or some other venue that might has nothing to do with my being a lawyer.

Side note: *Loop this lesson back to the earlier chapter where I talked about the importance of making sure people know you as more than just a lawyer. Now you can see that showing another side of yourself isn't just more interesting, it makes better business sense.*

My point is this: You want to build this list up as extensively as possible and *stay connected with these folks* so that they don't forget you. That way, when situations arise when they or people in their circle of influences *do* need a lawyer, they won't have to search the Internet or even give it all that much thought, because you will already be inside of their heads.

And just because their cases are finished and the verdicts have been reached doesn't mean you let them go. No, you keep their names on your list long after they've walked out that door.

How long should keep a client on your list? The running joke at

Ben Glass Law is until "You die, they die, or they move far away!"

It's funny, sure, but as with any humor, it's the truth within it that makes if funny, right?

Target Your Tribe

The minute you get those potential clients to look at your ad and raise their hands to say, "Send me your free report because I'd like to know more," they become members of your "tribe."

This is an important principle of GLM and stands at the center of what we call Direct Response Marketing (DRM). DRM is the new model.

Let's take a look at both:

The Old Model (Brand-building and Repetition)

This one is General Motors saying, "When you buy a car, think of us first."

In this case, the audience is massive, the message is generic, and the amount of money they're spending to reach this audience is, of course, *ridiculous*.

This is the giant GM getting and staying in the faces of its potential customers, hitting them time and time again, month after month, day after day, hour after hour, (sometimes minute after minute) with repetitive, brand-building ads that simply say, "We are GM. Buy our cars."

And if you're GM, of course, that's really all you need to say.

The New Model

Most solo and small firm lawyers obviously don't have this luxury or the resources to market with mass advertising. Some firms try, spending a ton of money "getting their name out there" for brand recognition. Mass TV, radio, and billboard advertising *can* work if you are the number one, two, or three spender in your area. There is a reason these media are used. Most of us aren't in that category. We want to invest in our practices efficiently.

This is when Direct Response Marketing (DRM) comes into play, and this is the type of marketing we practice at Ben Glass Law. *It works.*

Let me explain: In exactly the same way I emphasized to the pastors a few paragraphs up the importance of knowing who you are, what you're for, and what kind of a new audience you want to attract, the same principle applies here.

DRM requires you to offer something useful (and free) to the consumer to draw them in; a relevant piece of information or a useful white paper, say, on DUIs or divorce, or whatever your practice area is. Something that is useful to them that doesn't necessarily pitch your services but will still improve their lives in some way.

This is a lead generator. (A way cooler name for them is *widgets.*)

And when we can get them to raise their hands and make this request—*"Hey, send me that paper\"*—we've just changed the landscape. How? Because now I've been able to capture some important information about them (i.e., their email addresses and other contact information) *which gives me the opportunity to market directly to them.*

Bingo.

By using DRM, we achieve two major marketing goals at once. We can now identify our audience, then market directly to them.

A side note on "Call for a Free Consultation" advertising: Most lawyer advertising typically defaults to this strategy, but if you're one of those lawyers, resist the urge to have "call now" as the only response option for them. Remember, some consumers are not ready to talk to a lawyer yet. They may be "researching." They may just be afraid of us.

Instead, give the consumer something that will help them out and provide a useful resource they can use later. When you do this, you also create relationships that spring from giving them something useful with the expectation of nothing in return. And it establishes you as an expert on the subject; a trusted, go-to person with valuable information, knowledge, and resources.

GLM lawyers often refer to the "Call for the Free Consultation" advertising strategy as "a bridge too far." That's exactly what it is because some clients who need you are not ready to call for an appointment. Why take the chance?

So the magnet, in this case, is the piece of information that you offer that is interesting enough to make someone reach out and say, "Send it, please." This starts the conversation.

And that is what Magnetic Marketing® is all about.

The 70/30 Rule

This can be considered a subset to DRM. Listen up:

When lawyers think about their marketing budgets, they tend to ignore the fact that in a mature practice, seventy percent of revenue should come *from inside their own lists* of friends, former clients, and profession referral sources. Seventy percent!

Instead, they leap right into "doing it the old way, just because it's always been done that way," which is advertising to cold prospects.

Wrong move.

Your client list is your most important asset, so use it strategically and treat it like gold, because that's exactly what it is. It's gold. 70 percent of your time, energy, and money capital should be devoted to cultivating that "house" list.

Let me say it again: Your list is the most important marketing tool that you have.

Another Must: Solid Systems

Here's a mistake a lot of lawyers make. It's a mistake that I made for many years myself, so don't beat yourself up if you're doing it.

Here's the deal: Understand that your law practice should be used as a wealth-building tool. To be the best lawyer that you can be, invest in building and nurturing a solid system that does not require you, the lawyer and chief strategist, to spend time doing anything that is not the best use of your time.

Lots of lawyers assume that they're responsible for every single aspect of a client's case, at all times. That's old-school thinking.

The established bar has brainwashed lawyers into thinking this:

"Every one of my clients is unique. My clients expect me to be intimately familiar with every detail of their case, and as a good lawyer getting paid the big bucks, I absolutely *should* be on top of everything."

Here's the GLM approach: Create an internal system that frees you to do what your client has *paid* you to do, which is to be the chief strategist who is ultimately responsible for solving their problem. That is your primary job. (More on systems in a later chapter.)

Your second most important job is to create a system that ensures every aspect of your client's case is addressed...by the people who've been trained and put in place to address it.

As you build your system, make sure your tracking capabilities are top-notch too, so that if something goes wrong you have a system in place that points you towards asking the right questions.

Here's an example: An employee in client communication is found to not be doing what he's supposed to be. Having a good system in place would lead you to these important questions:

- Is there something in the system that needs correction?

- Have we properly communicated to the team our expectations of how the system is to be carried out?

- Is the team member properly following our directions?

Having this kind of system in place allows you to view your business from a more expansive perspective, and to figure out the most efficient way to solve problems when they occur.

Let me put it another way. When things go wrong, default to:

- Taking responsibility for the system you created

- Asking whether you have properly communicated how the system is to be executed

- Recognizing that you must fire employees who consistently demonstrate that they cannot execute your well-communicated instructions on how the system is to be executed

Relying on your system will help identify and fix the problem.

Ray Kroc Had it Right

The reason Ray Kroc was a genius and a visionary is because he saw that it was possible to put a system in place that would allow young, low-level, low-paid employees to make a good hamburger.

As simple as that.

Because of this system, McDonald's sells billions of hamburgers, all the time, in every corner of the world.

Some lawyers cringe when I compare them to McDonald's. I think you should get over it, but if you *don't* study McDonald's at least study Amazon, Apple, or Fed-Ex. Or any of the other billion-dollar plus companies out there who are following the basic principles of Ray Kroc's model.

I can guarantee a great result.

Kick the Nay-Sayers to the Curb

Whenever you break from the status quo—no matter what it is that you're breaking away from—the naysayers will come out in droves to distract (and detract) you from your mission.

Kick them to the curb.

I can pretty much guarantee you this: They will not understand this renegade new marketing system, nor will they want to take the time to try to.

Here are some of the comments that are bound to come your way. Hopefully, by reading them, you'll already know some of this nonsense when it comes your way.

Be ready to shut it all down.

What They'll Find Wrong with Your New Advertising Strategies and Marketing Principles

- *"No one's going to read all that dense copy. It needs more white space."*

- *"No one's going to take the time to read your white paper."* (Or your book or your newsletter, or any other piece of GLM-inspired marketing resources you try to share.)

- *"If you don't get on the phone **right now** to capture that client, you're going to lose them forever. They'll just go to the next lawyer in line."*

- *"Your idea will never work because it's never been done that way before."*

Or a modified version of the bullet above:

- *"I don't know anyone who's ever done it this way before."*

- *"The bar will never allow this."*

- *"That's way too expensive."*

Okay, so now you've been forewarned. But here's another option: If you decide to stick around and engage them in a discussion (God bless you for your patience) to really try to understand what they're trying to say, ask them this:

- *Have you ever built a successful business?* (I mean, why would I listen to anyone tell me how to market a law firm if they've never built a law firm themselves?)

- *Do you have other people you can point to who've followed your advice and who will resoundingly endorse your thinking? If so, can I speak with them?*

And I stole this next one from Dan Kennedy. I'm sure he won't mind my using it here—and these questions are directed to the people who are trying to do business with you:

- *If you're asking me to do business with you, give me the names of three other people you've done business with who would gladly do a deal with you again.*

- *Do you have followers who will resoundingly endorse you?*

. . .

I know, I know. If you haven't traveled this path before, there's really no way to tell whether any of this is going to work for you. I get that. It's a gamble.

It's natural to be skeptical about a belief system that tells you, *"You can design your life."* But beyond the skepticism lies something else—and this is what you should focus on: The indisputable fact that this stuff really does change lives.

You want a successful legal career and a healthy, balanced home life? Start with a set of rock-hard set of principles that guide your every move.

You already have them.

I just gave them to you.

SECTION III

LIVE THE LIFE YOU WANT TO LIVE

CHAPTER TEN
MAN NEEDS PHILOSOPHY

Decide to Decide

Okay, so you've seen the word *philosophy* in the title of this chapter and you're still holding this book in your hands. Good for you. Many lawyers would have bolted.

But you're still probably asking yourself, "Well, what *does* philosophy have to do with building a kick-ass practice and a thriving business?"

The question itself is legitimate—after all, our brains weren't trained for this stuff in law school—but the answer is even more legitimate.

Everything.

Yep, flip back a few pages and you'll see that I used that same bold statement in the previous chapter, when I asked the question, "What does marketing have to do with the business of law?"

It's the same answer, just a different question.

Having a set of pre-established values to guide your business, your practice, and your life is more than just important. It's essential. You can't get to a life of meaning, structure, and consistency without it. Your philosophy should stand at the core of everything you do. So when I throw out the question of what philosophy has to do with your personal and professional life, we bounce back to the very same answer:

Everything.

Listen up: Philosophy is simply an ordered way of thinking about the world and your unique place within it. It's a well-thought-out system of beliefs and principles that can guide you—and keep you—on the path to wellness, financial success, great legal marketing, and, yes, unimaginable happiness. Philosophy prevents you from making the same mistakes over and over.

You don't need me to tell you (but I will anyway, because it's important) that that path can get bumpy. Crap can come. Pitfalls and potholes can open up right in front of you and swallow you whole if you're not mentally prepared to deal with them *before* they arrive. Let's face it: Very bad things happen to very good people, all the time.

Here's the deal: Simply *reacting* to those pitfalls and potholes is just not going to cut it. That kind of passive, reflexive, non-thinking response to life and living just isn't good enough for an extraordinary life. Not only is it not good enough, it's exhausting. You deserve better.

What I'm about to say next might sound a little strange, but I promise you it's true: Choosing to live a life where you're only reacting to situations as they arise (i.e., letting life live *you* instead of you leading your life) is a principle in and of itself. It's a deliberate decision to live a life of chaos, confusion, and constant stress. Look around. This is the life most people live. Reacting rather than responding leads to a life that is, at best, average. You deserve better.

I'm going to swing back around to a point I made in the previous chapter, because it's also relevant here:

Where you are today is a product of the decisions you have made in the past, and where you'll be tomorrow will be a product of the decisions you made today.

If you do nothing else with this book other than deeply internalize that thought into your very being, then its purchase and the investment of the time it took to read it will be worthwhile.

In a world where the default is to blame someone else for where you find yourself today, this simple mindset "switch" to accepting responsibility for the ways your life is less than fulfilling and making a decision to change things will change your life.

So take the time to make the choices that are best for you, best for your business, and best for your family. If lawyers are ever to experience "wellness" in this profession, it must start with our philosophy of not blaming others.

Decide to decide to live your life and run your practice with purpose and precision. Build your life by building your principles. Then stick to them. Develop a rock-solid set of enduring values that will hold you steady in the storm and guide every aspect of your life and your practice, in both the good times and the bad.

Act. Don't just react.

Creating a carefully thought-out philosophy that you can weave throughout the fabric of your personal and professional life is no cakewalk. It won't happen overnight. It requires focus, commitment, and constant buy-in from you and your entire team. It requires you calling "timeout" from your overly busy life, escaping with pen and paper and thinking.

Let me be direct: It's hard as hell, especially as you're going through the process of identifying and building your values, but if it's better for you in the long-run, do you really want to worry about playing that "it's-too-much-work" card? If it wasn't hard, more lawyers would be happy.

In my life I get to hang out with a lot of very successful people running all sorts of businesses. There's not a one of them who think that what we entrepreneurs do is easy. Of my close friends who are successful entrepreneurs, I know that the vast majority devote considerable amounts of time working on the philosophical sides of their lives, either through book reading, small mastermind groups, or working with business coaches. In case you ever wondered, far more time is spent with a good business coach talking about the issues I raise in this book than talking about the next marketing tool.

Trust me.

Here's the good news: Developing a sound philosophy will happen once you decide you want it to happen.

Let me say one more thing about the importance of developing a philosophy. By definition, it will involve kicking all of your lazy thinking and low energy to the curb. This is what you'll have to do: Stand up. Stop sitting down. Quit letting others lead your life.

The actions that you take in life should not just be reactions.

There are exceptions, of course. When you touch a hot stove (or anything else that causes sudden pain or trauma), you'll automatically react by pulling your hand away. Smart move. That's your reptilian brain at work.

But what about all those other hours of the day when you're

not touching a hot stove? Those hours should be filled with careful thinking and deliberate behavior. Train your brain to slow itself down. Reflect. Ponder. Think. Hell, make the deliberate decision *not* to think. Each and every day, give your brain the break it needs to loosen up and think creatively. To do this, *get away from the grind of the office.* Teach yourself to take a walk instead. Most lawyers will object and say, "Oh, this won't work for me because my clients need to have access to me during business hours, and I've got to be available to them," or "See that pile of files over there? I need to get to them."

Those clients will be better served once you sharpen up your own saw. You can't serve your clients until you serve yourself, which means putting yourself first and stepping away from the grind each and every day for at least a few minutes. And don't do it randomly or whenever you think about it. Make it a priority and a pattern.

For me, this tends to be early morning kind of work. I'm an early riser, hitting CrossFit® at 5:30 a.m. about three or four times a week, but still getting up at that time most other mornings. When we are at the beach or on a cruise I have always been the first one up—reading and thinking—pondering "what if?"

You might be a night owl. Or you might be someone who can close the office door, put your feet up, and "just think" in the middle of the day. I can do that, but I confess I find it difficult when everyone else around me is working so hard. I feel guilty. I'm working on that. My "thinking time" is the most important thing I can do for myself, my family, my employees, and my clients. Busyness is no sign of success.

Ants are busy.

Dealing with clients and potential clients is an example of how we have deliberately thought out what types of habits are win-win for us and the clients.

At Ben Glass Law, we don't stress about the need to make ourselves available to our clients 24/7. Our plan is simple: We just don't do it. This is a *principle* of ours. It's a rule. It endures. We don't violate it. And guess what? It works.

Not only do we *not* believe in the 24/7 rule, we fight against it. We make time and *take* time every day to ask ourselves questions that most lawyers don't even consider. Questions like:

- "How do I want to maximize my life?"

- "How can I enhance my family's life?"

- "What sort of interactions should I be having with the people around me?"

- "How do I want to feel today?"

The more time you spend reflecting on questions like these in advance, the more likely it will be that when it's time to make an important decision or react to a challenging situation, your behavior, your thoughts, and the *pattern* of your thinking will come from a place of clarity, not chaos.

As long as you're pondering that, ponder this:

Every decision you make, personally or professionally, will influence the course of your life.

Knowing this, how could you *not* want to develop an enduring philosophy that stands at the center of your business, your practice, and even your marketing strategy? *You* determine the course of your life. Nobody else. It's on you. Change your life from the inside out. But you can't get this done by just flying by the seat of your pants. *This* is why man needs philosophy.

Hundreds of GLM lawyers from every discipline have already found what I hope you are actively looking for. This should tell you that it can be done, and that you can do it.

The first step is deciding to decide that you want it.

Decide you want it now.

A Pause and a Thank You

Before I go any deeper into this chapter, I need to pause. (We've established that pauses are important, right?) What I'm going to say *within* this pause might sound ridiculously obvious, but humor me. I want to say it:

If I'd never come to the realization that I needed an enduring set of principles to guide my business and my practice, I would not have them today.

What I'm trying to say is this: If my life hadn't intersected with the people who first introduced me to this kind of thinking, my principles would not be as solid as they are today. They might not even exist.

In this chapter in particular, I need to pause to pay homage to the brilliant author and visionary Ayn Rand. *Atlas Shrugged* and *The Fountainhead* were what first enlightened my thinking and turned on a lightbulb in my brain. My home library is filled with secondary "Rand" materials including one of my favorite annual reads, *I Am John Galt*, by Donald Luskin and Andrew Greta.

Read Ayn Rand's books. They might change your life. They did mine.

By the way, if you are not an Ayn Rand fan, save the hate mail unless you can tell me that you've actually read *Atlas Shrugged* and not just heard some politician or socialist rant against it. Heck, we have a podcast and video studio built into our law offices. Come by and we'll discuss!

Pause over.

Back to business.

Steps to Take, Points to Ponder, Stuff to Remember

Okay, it's time to get specific.

Here, I'll share a few of my philosophies about philosophy. My team and I have spent many long hours honing these values and principles, and I'll be honest: It's paid off, big-time.

Here's some solid stuff to ponder:

Building a Philosophy is a Living, Dynamic Process.

An enduring philosophy isn't defined by a shiny plaque on the wall or a two-day, off-site retreat with your team (although these things can certainly be helpful tools). A philosophy has to exist in your DNA, as a living, breathing thing. And even though it's alive, *you should never let it grow old.*

At Ben Glass Law, we work hard to make sure our values and philosophies always feel fresh, even though they were developed years ago. *If you're going to live by them, you've got to keep them alive.* They must always feel relevant; never outdated or stale.

Once you've developed a set of core principles, don't get lazy. Decide to decide to keep them alive. Don't get tripped up into thinking that once you've created these principles, the process is over.

Far from it. Things are just beginning.

And here's even more good news:

If you do it right, the process never, ever ends.

Your Philosophy Belongs to You. Own It.

I'll say it again: Building a set of core values is no easy feat. That doesn't mean that you can't do it; it just means that it's going to take effort—and nobody's going to do it for you.

You are the one to decide and determine your own trajectory and your own set of principles. In the same way that you are the author of your own story, you are also the creator of your own core values. Nobody else can create them for you.

Two great reads on discovering and then living your core value are Verne Harnish's *Scaling Up* and Jim (*Good to Great*) Collins' *Beyond Entrepreneurship*. These books were very instrumental to our leadership team at Ben Glass Law.

Don't Lead Your Life by Whim.

Since I've used these words before, let me put it like this: Be brave enough to think deeply and deliberately. Don't fall into the trap of responding to life passively, reacting to situations as they unfold. Living like this is stressful and frightening. Again, it is exhausting. Resist the urge.

Average people respond to situations based solely on the emotions they happen to be experiencing at the moment without taking time to think things through in advance. Be more purposeful than that. Take the time to take the time. It works.

Here's an example: As a soccer referee, I spend a lot of time anticipating how other people might respond to the decisions I make and the actions I take when I'm out on the field.

While I don't have the time or the desire to try to *control* their actions, I *am interested* in being thoughtful and deliberate if a stressful situation should come up. (And believe me, somebody is always going to be dissatisfied with a soccer referee's decisions. Somebody's always going to find fault with one of my calls. It's the nature of the job.)

But I find that when I think things through in advance, when I try to anticipate my reaction to events *before* they unfold, it really helps to slow my brain down. This gives me time to map out a strategy in advance, so that when something does go down (on the soccer field or off) I'm able to rise above my own emotions and come at the situation from a place of reason and, yep, relative calm. If I lived my life by whim, none of that would be possible.

Insist on Total Buy-In. No Half-Stepping Allowed.
Here's How it Works at Ben Glass Law.

We have nine core values that make up our overall philosophy, and every single decision we make springs from these core values. There's a plaque that hangs on the wall that lists those values. They *should* stay in our face every single day because they stand at the center of our practice and they guide every decision we make. Here they are:

1. We serve the client.

2. We do the right thing.

3. We believe in respect.

4. We practice open, timely communication.

5. We empower through education.

6. We solve problems.

7. We strive to understand people.

8. We are forever learners.

9. We don't play games.

Living by these values allows us to act—not just react—to everything that we encounter in a way that is thoughtful, consistent, and carefully thought-out ahead of time. The simple truth of the matter is this: Having a core philosophy that weaves itself through every aspect of the business just helps us get to better answers. It helps us lead better lives. It acts an emotional enhancer and not a detractor.

Here's the rub, though: Any law firm can hang a plaque on their wall and any lawyer can talk the talk. But unless you mean what you say and follow it up with action, unless you walk the walk and *live by* the values and principles you've worked so hard to create, you're wasting your time.

My team knows the drill: When it comes to abiding by the principles, no half-stepping is allowed. No exceptions. We push ourselves every day to remain consistent to our values. Like I said earlier, it's become a part of our DNA. Anything less will not do.

Okay, so you already know that your business life consumes a huge part of your daily existence. It is the source of your financial security and the primary means of providing for and protecting your highest priority; your family.

So why *wouldn't* you want to make this overall experience the very best that it can be? Why *wouldn't* you do everything in your power to make sure that these practices and principles create a strong enough foundation to guide every business decision you make? This is important stuff.

Decide to make it your top priority. No excuses.

Make Them Smile.

I have a little game I like to play with myself every day. I call it a "challenge of the heart." Whenever I encounter anyone I don't know—the cashier at the grocery store, the waiter who brings me my meal, the crew who cleans my offices—I always want to try to make them smile. Who knows? It might be the only chance they've had to smile all day.

Yep, this is a philosophy. For me, it's an enduring value and a daily goal.

Let's loop this principle back to the law. One of our goals at Ben Glass Law? Try to understand people first, then try to create joy in their lives. It's a pretty simple formula. Whether it's a client, a vendor, a lawyer, or the guy who puts up the drywall in our new suite of offices, we always try to do or say something that's going to somehow make their lives *just a little bit better.*

I see it as a *win-win*: I feel good when I can make someone smile—whether I know them or not—and I know for a fact that it makes them feel good, too.

A principle doesn't always have to be about business, then—but if it's solid and well-thought-out, it will enhance your business in unimaginable ways. Being kind is not only an important principle:

It's also good business.

"Those Ben Glass Lawyers are Really Friendly!"

When we moved into our new offices in the fall of 2018, just about every vendor, contractor, and tech expert we considered hiring said, "We hate working with lawyers. We don't know if we want to take this job on."

No joke.

Here's how I responded, "But we're not *like* all the other lawyers! We'll be the friendliest people you've ever met!"

And we were.

We ended up forming great relationships with the vendors and contractors who helped build out our new offices. Every time an issue came up, they bent over backwards to solve the problem and make it better than we ever could have expected, without any stress or drama or rancor. And we, in turn, treated them with the same amount of respect and kindness.

It's sad to say, but you know as well as I do that this kind of behavior is rare for lawyers.

When they were finished with their work, what we heard was, "Those Ben Glass lawyers sure are friendly!" That's what I'd call a happy, unexpected moment.

Let's loop it back to the law. Being kind to others, whether it's a juror, a client, a judge or the guy that cleans the courtroom at the end of the day, should be the norm rather than the exception. For us, it is.

Ben's Philosophy

I wake up every day determined to inspire others to live life big and to accept and be proud of the fact that they are endowed by our Creator with certain gifts and talents that are unique to them.

My message to lawyers is this: *You have a role in all of this, too. You should be sharing your gifts and talents with others. If you're not sharing your talents, start. If you're already doing it, keep up the good work (and thank you)!*

Inspiring other people is one of my gifts, and I'm going to do everything I can to use that gift to help others. What's more, I'm okay with saying this! I'm comfortable with it and unembarrassed by it. I talk about it all the time—in my books, in my training seminars, and whenever I speak to outside groups. This, too, is a part of my DNA.

You, too, should try to be an inspiration to those around you. You worked your ass off to get through law school, worked to get to exactly where you are today, so you've obviously got a light to shine. Everyone does. When you refuse to shine that light (or you never even realized that you *should* be shining it), other people are prevented from enjoying and benefitting from it.

We are more than just lawyers. We are inspirers, too. Or at least we should be.

Let me ask you this: When did you last hear a lawyer say, in answer to a young person's question about pursuing the law as an occupation, "That's terrific, the world needs more people like you to be lawyers?" I've heard the question and I've listened to the answers others give for years. Almost without fail the Eeyores of our profession cast doubt on the dreams of the young person.

That's sad. Eeyore, "please go home."

Take Time—No, MAKE Time— to Step Away From Your Business

We've touched on this one already, but here I want to dig a little deeper by asking an easy question:

When does most of your creative thinking occur?

I can tell you this: It's not while you're sitting in a deposition or finishing a brief or starting a conference call with your client. Your brain is at its best when it's most relaxed, when it's emptied out and free of distraction. (Think singing in the shower. Walking in the woods. Or falling into a super deep REM sleep.) In other words: When you're *away from the office*.

Let me ask another question:

What's the secret to dramatically increasing your income? (Now I've got your attention.)

Here's the answer: By spending less time at the office. By standing up and walking away from the office to give your brain a break. Doing it this way is called *militant time management,* and it works. But to make it work you've got to say no to the time-wasters. (Dan Kennedy calls these "time vampires." Right on.)

Taking time to contemplate and refresh your thinking isn't high up on the list of priorities for most lawyers. In fact, it isn't on the list at all. Most lawyers think it's a mistake to take these kinds of "leisurely" breaks during office hours. They don't realize that it's *not* only not productive to work all the time, it's harmful, too—and not a great business decision.

Look at your own situation: Where are you when you're feeling most relaxed? I can bet it's not at the office. So doesn't this automatically point to the fact that your best thinking occurs some-where else? Think about it.

If you already know ahead of time that your most creative thinking occurs when your brain is relaxed and removed from the office environ-ment, then why the hell wouldn't you create the opportunity to step away on a regular basis?

Try it. (And don't cheat: Falling asleep in front of the TV doesn't count as "creative time" because you're simply responding to your own exhaustion. Give it more effort.)

Go on a walk (and do it in the middle of the workday). Find a park or a quiet place and go sit in it. Figure out how to break your brain away from the business.

At Ben Glass Law, we take this seriously. We've learned to say "no" to the time-wasters, whether that time-waster is a colleague or social media or unscheduled call from a client. Check out our internal mantra:

"The less I do, the more I make."

Consider this analogy:

How CrossFit® Promotes Creative Thinking

The strength and endurance I receive from doing CrossFit® doesn't come from the hour of stimulus I receive while doing the "workout of the day." It comes from the rehabilitative, restful time after that hour of stimulus, when new neural pathways are created and new cells are generated.

This can be said of any type of exercise. You don't lose weight or gain strength *while you're exercising.* All of that good stuff happens when your body is at rest. The same principle applies to your mental condition: Your brain needs time to rejuvenate and recover if it's going to get stronger. By definition, then, we must take time to slow our thinking and get away from the grind of the office.

The Fifteen-Minute Challenge

Try this: For a full week, in fifteen-minute increments, record everything you do and every action you take. List everything—even the small stuff. Then review it at the end of the day. You'll be surprised to see how much time you've eaten up with unnecessary distractions and the greedy time vultures.

Want to make it even more challenging? Find an accountability partner—someone you can share your findings with at the end of each day. I promise you this exercise will increase your productivity. Why? Because you'll want to show your partner that you spend your time productively—not watching cat videos on YouTube or playing solitaire or posting on Facebook. Remember: This is time you'll never get back. Treat it as the precious commodity that it is.

Be militant about it.

Piano Lessons

Way back when we had only had four children (not the nine we have today), I decided to step out of my comfort zone and take piano lessons. A few of my kids were taking lessons, so I just jumped in with them.

I'd never taken lessons, of course. I knew nothing about playing or reading music. *But I was curious, and I wanted to learn.* I'd play along with them at their recitals (with all the other children) and nope, I wasn't very good, but guess what?

By stepping outside of my comfort zone, I learned something new. And I also sent the message to those other young students that even big guys like me ("old" guys is probably how they'd put it) can try something different, even if it's hard. And I probably inspired at least a few of the parents to push themselves past their own self-imposed limits.

Nope, I wasn't very good at playing, but that didn't matter.
I wanted to try anyway.

Design Your Environment

Okay, so you've made the commitment to block off time at work
to push yourself *away* from work. Now mark it on your calendar
and stick to it. *Honor your commitment. Make your team honor it, too.*
This is really all about designing your environment, making
good choices, then insisting on adherence and buy-in from everyone
around you. If it's on your schedule to take a walk at 10:00 a.m.,
then take the damn walk at 10:00 a.m.! Don't be distracted by the
colleague who drags you into a drawn-out discussion at 9:55 or
the client who makes an unscheduled call at 9:58, as you're leaving.

Making this commitment and insisting on complete buy-in
from everyone around you also speaks to a much larger principle:
Integrity. Maintain your integrity by doing what you say you're
going to do. Make the decisions you need to make about how you're
going to expend your energy. Designing your life means mapping
out the moments in your day.

Dan Kennedy calls this "scripting," and it's a biggie. Let it
become a principle. A rule. An enduring value. And once you do,
don't let anyone or anything knock you off your game. Stick to it.
Script it.

Change Your Choices

Years ago, when I thought that being a great lawyer meant doing
what all of the other lawyers were doing, I'd attend an annual
lawyer association conference—and I wouldn't miss a year. I never
thought that CLE in fifteen to thirty minute segments made any
sense, but hell, everyone in the association was there, so this must

be what good lawyers do to build better practices.

Turns out that that these conferences, like most held around the country, had very little to do with building better practices. Nothing startlingly new or groundbreaking was ever covered at these conferences and the only reason I kept attending year in and year out was because, well, that's the way we'd always done it!

But about twenty years ago, which is when I started to really develop an interest in Dan Kennedy's philosophies and practices, I saw that he offered an annual conference for entrepreneurs at around that same time. This presented a scheduling conflict, of course.

Funny thing: That scheduling conflict helped change the trajectory of my life.

I can still remember driving home from my very last major lawyer's conference. I was cruising down Interstate 64 in Virginia, kicking myself for having made the choice *not* to attend Dan's conference (which I knew had to be more exciting). I remember how miserable I was.

But I also remember the very moment—still speeding down I-64, mind you—when I decided, "Never again."

Never again would I attend the lawyer's conference simply because that's the way I'd always done it.

Never again would I sit around listening to lawyers complain about unfair judges, missed recitals, crappy clients, and, on the golf course, crappy drives. I'd had it up to here (visualize me holding my hand up to my chin) with sob stories about neglected families and frustrated spouses.

No more.

I never went back. Instead, I started going to Dan's annual conference for entrepreneurs, which was, frankly, much more expensive than the lawyer conferences . . . and it changed my life.

At the business-building conferences there were few lawyers but many men and women from every industry, cross-breeding their ideas, sharing philosophies, and challenging each other to think more deeply. The contrast was startling. I had found *my* place!

I realize now that it was this contrast that really gave me courage—and I'm not just talking about the contrast between the styles of the two conferences, but the contrast between the *philosophies between the two groups.*

It didn't take long to shift my thinking to another place. It didn't take me long to begin the work of building a set of core principles and being brave enough to stick to them, no matter what.

So I moved from barreling down Interstate 64 (miserable and frustrated) to walking an entirely different path altogether.

It's a path to wellness, and I'll follow it for the rest of my life. But it's way, way more than just a path.

It's an enduring philosophy.

CHAPTER ELEVEN
SCALE UP. NOW.
USE YOUR SYSTEMS TO BUILD THE LIFE YOU REALLY WANT.

Here's a little secret:

Turns out that figuring out how to bring new clients through the door is a relatively easy task. Once you unravel a few important principles, figure out in what order things need to get done, and commit to ruthless execution of the steps, it won't be all that hard to bring in new business. Our members prove this every day.

Before we go dive any further into this chapter, though, let's check under the hood for a second. Let's do a quick tune-up that consists of two parts (well, three, really) to unpack what we've learned so far. And I can give you a hint: The third point has to do with scaling, and it's a biggie. But first let's bring everything together in a way that makes the most sense.

Before we get to number three, let's review numbers one and two.

I want all of this to be as straightforward as possible, because this is important.

Here's our two-point plan so far. This is the stuff we already know:

1. Build a kick-ass marketing strategy based on direct response principle.

2. Build the *foundation* for that marketing strategy—lead generation magnets (books, reports, white papers), a database that will automate follow-up for new leads, and a monthly printed newsletter before you spend any other money on marketing.

At Ben Glass Law, we've been doing both things for years, and doing both things very well; well enough to teach it to other lawyers how to do it.

So these two points represent the core of the core.

But now, to the nitty-gritty. This is where it gets good.

There's more to the core.

There's a third element to this equation that really loops everything together. Listen up:

3. Putting smart, sound *systems* in place is the only way to ensure that your business grows into the best business it can possibly be.

And by that, I mean this:

You can build the best legal practice the world has ever known. You can also build the strongest foundation in the world, with the sharpest people, the best product, and the coolest marketing. But if you don't know how to *scale that business,* you will be toast in our fast-moving, ever changing economy. Those who plan on practicing law the same way in five years as they are doing today will be left behind. Today's consumer drives the market. Simple as that.

If you want your business to thrive and to grow, you've got to have a system in place that will *accommodate* growth and change. And no, the answer is not just hiring more people. Simply throwing more people at a problem will rarely help you grow smartly.

To keep up with tomorrow's legal market, you've got to *scale up*. You've got to *know how to grow*.

I'll be the guinea pig again.

I mentioned earlier that I started my law practice with two people: Me and one assistant—my sister. I handled every aspect of every case. As I learned more about marketing—and once I got really good at it—the situation changed.

Business started growing. More and better (bigger) cases. That's what happens when you have a sound marketing plan: You've now identified and reached out to your avatar, created marketing that speaks to him, and you've created an interesting and differentiating message that prompts them to reach out to you first. (Remember? Information marketing. Long follow up. Database. Newsletter.) This brings you more of cases you want. The ones you are good at handling. The people you like to represent.

Don't misunderstand: Figuring out the smartest way to make sure your business consistently operates at the top of its game and deciding how best to accommodate your growth is a damned good problem to have but it *is* challenging. More stuff they didn't teach you in law school. Businesses that don't figure out how to "scale up" can crash in their "success."

There's a way to go about growing your business that is deliberate and strategic. Always remember that this should be a purposeful process, not a random, fly-by-the-seat-of-your-pants deal.

Hell, *knowing that you're growing* should be fun and exciting because it puts you in rarified air: small business success. For lawyers, it's really rarified air: you can be one of the few who loves what it is we do, makes good money, and isn't destroying their family in the process. Look around and ask questions of your peers. My point is that you can have fun with this stuff and be smart about it at the same time. The two things aren't mutually exclusive. You can do both, and I'm getting ready to show you how.

Before I do, though, let's bounce back to Ben for a second. Let's swing back to the Ben whose business was growing so fast he could barely keep up.

As more cases started flowing in, it became impossible for me to take in all the additional work—at least not without compromising the quality of the service that my current clients were accustomed to and my new clients were certainly going to expect based on what they had heard about me. Something had to give.

I knew enough to know that I couldn't keep taking on all the additional cases without making some kind of major change, and I knew I needed to make the right decisions. Everything was riding on this. The next steps I took could either make or break my firm.

Breaking was not—and never will be—a viable option, though at times it seemed that I was trying mightily to break it!

This was my challenge:

I needed to figure out a way to deliver the same high-quality legal services to a larger number of clients without having to be continually involved in every single aspect of the business. This is what scaling is all about. You see, as the business gets bigger the management of that business gets more complex. The people and systems that get you to, say, a million dollars a year are never the same as those that get you to three to five million (or more—one of our GLM members has revenues of over $15 million with a regional based Social Security practice.)

In fact, this *is* scaling.

And if you don't figure out how to do it, your practice will likely be an eternal source of frustration for you.

Scaling your business—keeping it tightly run, carefully balanced, inherently flexible, and always poised for growth and/ or to tackle challenges—this is how you set yourself up to win the race. If you can get this part right, if you can figure out a way to get your arms around the actual process of building an internal "fallback" system that guides every aspect of your business, and do it in a way that keeps you from having to do everything, all the time—then you're ready to run this race. And win.

Not only are you prepared to win, but because you've decided to put a good, solid internal system in place, you've also just figured out a way to *keep on winning* all the races that are ahead of you. Why? Because with a set of systems intact, you've just bumped up the rules of the game.

What I'm trying to say is this: By putting a kick-ass marketing system in place, and implementing that plan consistently, you've put yourself in the big leagues.

But don't take your victory lap too early. There's still work that needs to be done and steps that need to be followed. Here I want to offer up three important points about scaling. And if you can get these right, you will change the entire trajectory of your life. I promise.

Want to build a good system? Here's how to do it three steps.

How to Scale: A Three-Part "Quick" List

1. **Get everybody on the same page.**

We've touched on this one before; the context is just a little different. To make sure everybody's on the same page, it's imperative that everyone understand why your firm is even in the market. Why do you exist? Hold your team accountable for asking the following questions:

- *What do we want this practice to look like?* This is as much about having a clear-sighted vision and an enduring philosophy as it is about having a solid business and marketing plan. Everybody should have the same answer about what the practice should look like because *you* made this decision already and then *you* hired and trained to *that* vision. Anyone not on the right bus? That's your fault and you need to fix it.

- *Who is our avatar and why are we the best for that person?* I once heard a lawyer at a regular lawyer meeting profess that he was not any different from any of the other personal injury lawyers out there so he could not figure out what "different message" to use in his marketing.

  Sad. Better for that lawyer to have already been either running a business in another industry or working for someone else. Anyone that does not firmly believe that they are the perfect choice for someone doesn't even deserve a seat at the table. How could his team be "on the same page" with him when he wasn't on any page at all himself? He was just existing. The dinosaurs just "existed." Then they didn't.

- *What are two to three things that you do that are important to the mission of the firm and how will we measure improvement?*

It is a good exercise to, every once in a while, have each of your team members write out on one page exactly what it is they do for you each day. If you haven't done this in a while, you might find a gap between what you think they should be doing and what they are actually doing while getting paid by you each day. You also might find that some of them are doing things that are, in fact, valuable to the team, but you didn't even know they were doing. This is "initiative." We like "initiative."

The object of this exercise is two-fold: first, do you have each of your team members doing work that uses their highest gifts and talents? The closer the match there the better for everyone. Second, of the things they are doing that match their gifts and the firm's needs, how can we measure what they are doing so that we can determine if there is improvement over time?

Although this is not a business management book, per se, here is a thought from my friend, Clate Mask, CEO of Infusionsoft, that is worth pondering.

> *"Where performance is measured, performance improves. Where performance is measured and reported, performance improves dramatically. Where performance is measured and reported publicly, performance improves exponentially."*

As I mentioned, getting your entire team onto the same page is important, but it's also tricky. *Keeping* them on the same page is even trickier, because the very act of ensuring your business is moving in the right direction requires change in and of itself—sometimes a change in the direction (when, for example, a legislature wipes out a practice area, as has happened in medical malpractice and worker's compensation in some states), and often a change in the people who will help get you to the next level.

The act of scaling is, by its very definition, a systematic process.

It requires your visioning of the future (remember, different brain than your lawyer brain) and consistent buy-in from everyone on your team, which requires your business leadership (again, different brain).

As a leader, you must constantly be asking the three questions I just asked a few paragraphs up. This is not "one and done" stuff. Yes, it is challenging. Yes, it is different from what you may have thought about what it takes to run a law firm. Yes, it causes pain, sometimes. I hate firing people when the reason is "we are growing and we have hit the limit of your talents, so you must go." Yes, you'd probably be more comfortable just doing the lawyer stuff.

All I can tell you is that there are reasons why some law firms, in any practice area you can name, kill it, while others get killed. Why twenty percent of solo and small firms do very well (with "very well" defined not just by money but by living life exactly the way the owner(s) want to live life). What we are talking about is hard work. That's why, way back at the beginning of this book, I talked about "true ambition."

Here's the deal: My team knows where I want to take the firm. We have open and honest discussions about that. And it's up to me to build systems that attract great clients and great people to service those clients. So now let's talk about getting great people.

2. Get great people.

This one is tricky, too. The people on your team who operate to get you to one level of your business will not be the same people who will (or who can) get you to that next level. This "law" is as true as gravity.

Remember what I just said about the lawyers out there who aren't interested in winning the race? The same can apply to some of the people in your organization, too. It's just not in everyone's DNA to grow and/or to get better.

Keep this in mind: Different people have different skill sets, desires, goals, and interest levels—and guess what? That's the way it should be! Not everyone has the same drive as you and I do.

At the end of the day, you've got to do what's right for you and what's best for your business. Period. If what you're asking someone to do at the next level is something they're just not capable of doing, then that puts additional bad stress on them, on you *and* on your business, and bad stress is never, ever the right choice. (Testing someone's limits creates stress, too, but this is the kind of stress from which life decisions for both you and them will be made. If there isn't some stress around the office you aren't doing your job as leader.)

Don't be afraid to be selfish. Here's what drives me in the business decisions I make each and every day—even (maybe especially) when the decision involves a member of your team who might need to be reassigned or let go:

It has to be good for me and I want it to be good for you. It has to be good for me first, but if for you (the employee) this place isn't the place to secure for your family the financial and emotional security that you need, then you must, for your life, make the change that suits you.

Everybody has to understand this principle, because it's what drives the firm forward and it is what drives lives forward. Compromising this principle in any way—by any one—puts the firm in reverse. I'm not interested in going backward, and I will not do it. We only want to be in drive, moving forward. Never, ever in reverse.

But back to the person who might not be able to grow with the company: If they understand the underlying principles of why and how you're running the law firm, and they understand that they can no longer fill the role of helping you get there, *and* they understand that you are willing to help them find the next great place for them, then that helps. No, this isn't easy, but it's right.

And we always go with right. Even when right is difficult.

A side note about systems: *Systems are more important than the people who run them. People are free to come and go and they will, for all of the reasons I just talked about. Systems, by definition, must endure. They are the hub of the wheel; the people are the spokes; necessary, but interchangeable.*

The Case of Mary

Here's what I mean about systems and people: Say I'm talking with a lawyer who's describing a member of his team and I hear, "Oh, we just love Mary. She's been with me for twenty-five years! She's the only one who knows every detail about running this business!" Well, about a million red flags go up in my mind.

My reaction is, "Dude! Mary is a liability, not an asset. The fact that she's been a part of your team for a quarter of a century is *touching*, sure, but if she's the only one who knows every detail about your business, you're putting yourself in grave danger."

What happens if Mary gets sick one day? Or maybe she splits town because her husband got a new job in another state? That's way too much risk for a small law firm. Something's got to shift.

Here's the deal: You cannot allow your law firm to become that vulnerable. This is why systems trump people, harsh as that may sound if quoted out of context. Mary should not be the hub of the wheel.

Mary should be the spoke. And one of many, at that.

· · ·

Ideally, you want to have good people and good systems in place. That's obviously the best combination. But if you have to choose between the two, choose systems.

Systems should always win out.

This leads me to the most important task of all:

3. Get a great system

When something falls through the cracks in your business—a misstep, an overlooked detail, a mistake with a client—don't turn to the person who let it happen. Remember our default mindset: where you are today is a result of the decisions you have made in the past. When mistakes are made in the office, turn to the system you created to fix the problem first.

If you have a system in place and somebody drops the ball, here are the questions to be asked, in this order:

- Do we have the right system in place so that this problem that just now happened will not happen?

- Have we communicated the system well? Has the person who dropped the ball been trained to execute the system flawlessly system?

- Do we have the right person sitting in the right seat on the bus to execute the system?

Accurate answers to those three questions will tell you exactly what you need to do next, which is either:

- Fix the system.

- Communicate the steps in the system more clearly (retrain the employee).

- Get a different person in that seat.

Here's the cool thing: As uber-leader of your firm, *you* are not the one who has to come up with new and improved systems and or training on systems. You should always be asking your team, "What are your ideas for making the system better?" and, "Where does our system feel most vulnerable? Are we okay where we are, or do we need to look at a redesign?"

Let me say it again: Your system should always be the hub of the wheel.

Never, ever should it be the spoke.

The Sad Truth about Systems

Okay, so I guess I don't have anything all that sad (or bad) to say about systems. The sad part is that there are so few places where lawyers can go to learn about them.

It's not like there are a ton of seminars on legal systems for solo and small law firms. My friend, John Fisher, a medical malpractice attorney in New York, has written a great book on the subject, *The Power of a System*, where he lays out in great detail exactly what works for him and invites you to take and modify what will work for you. I recommend John's book.

My question is this: Why would anybody be afraid to put into place a process that guarantees that when something is repeated in your office, it's repeated to your high standards, *all the time*?

If the action produces positive results, the system should be designed to automatically repeat them. If the action produces negative results, something's wrong with the system. It needs to be fixed.

I mentioned Michael Gerber in an earlier chapter—the best-selling author and renowned small business *evolutionary*. Here's Gerber's deal: You should always be building systems in your business that would permit the business to be franchised and then run by others.

It's kind of like what I was saying earlier, when we were looking at the young Ben trying to accommodate his growing business: If I'd continued to try to work on every single aspect of every single incoming case, I wouldn't have grown: I'd have fallen flat, because I couldn't sustain the volume and the high quality at the same time.

So I *had* to put a system in place that freed me up to be what my clients hired me to be: The chief strategist on their case. I can't be a strategist and a legal researcher or a brief writer at the same time. And it's stupid for me to try.

How to Scale Up Successfully: Ben Shares a Perfect Example.

There are plenty of ways to do this thing wrong. Listen to the perfect example of how we did it right.

In our ERISA long-term disability practice we were faced with a challenge: If we were to get more cases, we needed to bring in more writers because each case required a lot of highly detailed, highly focused writing. (Think long appeals and even longer briefs.)

ERISA work is a very niche practice and there aren't a lot of lawyers in that area. I thought it would be impossible to ramp up this part of our business—not without a huge influx of top-notch attorney-writers familiar with ERISA law, which is rare—so I turned to Samy Chong and talked it through.

Samy convinced me that this wasn't impossible at all, or at least we didn't have clear evidence that this was impossible. He told me I needed to start visualizing this practice area working out and what it would look like when built "perfectly" and that, once I had clearly visualized the desired outcome, I needed to start talking to people about what exactly I was looking for. (Samy calls this "telling the universe what you need.")

Shortly after my conversation with Samy, I attended a local mastermind group (more on that in the next chapter) and one of the lawyers who heard me explaining my need for good ERISA writers asked me if I'd ever heard of a group called the "Military Spouse JD Network?" These are lawyers who are the spouses of folks in the military. Because they're always transferring from state to state with their spouses, it's very difficult for them to get a license in each state.

I hadn't, of course, which only piqued my interest. So I did my research, learned more about the group. Then we created an ad that solicited these lawyers (as outside contractors rather than full-time staff) and it was unbelievable how many solid, well-qualified, experienced lawyers we got as a result. (I don't think most realize how many great lawyers are out there waiting to be tapped for their talents, and who really, really want—and need—the work.)

When we ran that ad, the responses came pouring in. It's one of the best business decisions I've ever made. Why? Because it gave us the ability to scale up—fairly quickly, too—*and* keep our internal system fully intact. We already *had a system* in place for running the cases through, but *now we had more of the right people to help us work these all these new cases.*

This is a perfect example of how a scale-up works: You know your practice, you know your purpose, you have a system in place that works, and you bring in the right people to get the job done.

Voila. The perfect combination.

Here's what happened next: Our ERISA practice quadrupled. As of this writing, it's about to quintuple, and we're still going strong. Strong enough so that we taught a seminar in June 2019 that took a deep dive into systems creation that summarizes how we were able to quintuple the size of our ERISA practice in record speed. Other lawyers are eager to hear how we were able to grow this part of the practice so fast, and we are eager to share the information. (By the way, lawyers paid up to $12,500 to attend this day-and-a-half seminar, and we didn't even offer CLE credit. This shows that you don't need to force lawyers into mandatory CLE classes—you need to offer them something that will actually change their lives!)

. . .

All of this information on systems speaks directly to the need to provide *a consistently high-quality client experience whose delivery is not totally dependent on you.* When you get this right, the rules of the road will expand in a way you've never even imagined. The race will be yours to win.

So grab the keys to the Ferrari.

You've got a race to win.

CHAPTER TWELVE
THE POWER OF THE MASTERMIND

My buddy Bill Glazer has a saying that hits me right in the heart. It packs such a punch because it applies directly to me. Every time I hear it, I think, *Right on. I'm not in this alone after all.*

Bill says it best:

An entrepreneur is the loneliest person in the world.

If you're an entrepreneur, *you get this.* You can definitely relate.

But even if you don't *feel* like an entrepreneur, this chapter will still feel relevant because I'm talking to *any* solo or small-firm attorney who knows what the pressure of providing for and protecting your family feels like. And this can be a very lonely journey because no one "in the establishment" cares a whit about your *business* struggle. They are there begging you to "give more" of your hours and your time to *their* causes but no one is there, late at night, sitting at your kitchen table with your spouse, trying to figure out *your* business.

If you're holding this book in your hands, chances are you feel the weight of either owning or running a law firm on your shoulders, too. You know the ups and the downs, the fears, and the doubts that can creep in through the tiniest cracks to gnaw away at your very soul.

Sure, running your own business is rewarding as hell, not to mention a huge source of personal and professional pride, but Bill's still got it right: That stranded-on-a-desert-island kind of loneliness can make you feel like you're the only person with these struggles in the world.

Fortunately, it doesn't have to be that way. There's a very cool solution.

Your loneliness is only an option; you are not *required* to feel that way. You can make the deliberate decision—decide to decide, as you've heard me say before—to feel something other than loneliness. That's what I did. And though I didn't realize it at the time, I discovered this strategy by accident in law school, well before I was deep into the science of marketing, advertising and building a business.

What happens when you bring a group of people together with similar goals and interests? Who share their ideas, their knowledge, and their experiences with each other in a way that creates a larger group consciousness?

This is the power of the mastermind, and it's probably the strongest power you've ever experienced, because it's bigger than you. As I mentioned, this is the power that comes from bringing together like-minded people who, through brainstorming, studying, and/ or exchanging ideas and information, become stronger as a group than they are by themselves.

Dan Kennedy turned me on to Napoleon Hill and Hill turned me on to the concept of the mastermind in his book, *Think and Grow Rich,* when he made the observation that back in his day, one of the secrets to success was for entrepreneurs to hang out together. Share ideas for success. Hold each other accountable. Tap into each other's thoughts.

> **Note:** *I had actually seen and tried to read* Think and Grow Rich *many years earlier but because the concepts were so foreign to me and because there was no one else I knew at that time who knew who Hill was, let alone had read the book, I put it aside.*

Your success has as much to do with your mindset and your thinking as it does with your business strategy or your marketing plan. (You should know by now, because I've said it so many times, that your philosophy and your thinking are what should *determine* your marketing. The two things are closely connected.)

This is what I learned from Hill: That it is right, it's good, and it's smart to hang out with people (not just lawyers) who think like we do; who have the same entrepreneurial mindset as you do; who can converse openly and honestly with you (and each other) in a way that people "on the outside" simply don't understand; and who can call you out on your B.S. by holding you accountable for the things you say and the actions you take (or don't take).

By "thinking like we do," I mean thinking like those of us who believe that America is the greatest country on earth and we are blessed to live here; that this is the land of unlimited opportunity; that where you started has very little influence on where you can end up; that your decisions, and yours alone, map out your life; and that yes, as you become more and more successful and craft the life you want to live, there will be people who want to show off their ignorance, bring you down to their level to engage in their drama rather than do the work necessary to free up their own lives, and you should ignore their chirping.

In a mastermind group, traditional thinking goes right out the window. One plus one does not equal two. Depending on how you look at it or what theory you want to advance, it could equal five. Or maybe nine. A single idea can change the trajectory of your life. I've described it before as an "explosion" of thoughts and ideas.

As part of my pattern, I make it my business to either attend or host a mastermind group on a regular basis. You should consider it, too—but make it a habit rather than a one or two-time thing. There are bright, innovative entrepreneurs out there who are either waiting for you to join their group or waiting for you to start one. Go ahead and try it.

To start, all you have to do is, well, start.

Once you've made the decision to do it, then what the hell—do it!

I did it and it changed my life.

A Mastermind Group: The Early Version

At the beginning of the book I described how, as a student in law school, I depended on my study groups to help carry me through. I made a point of hanging out (and studying with) fellow students who were smarter than me and who could explain difficult concepts to me. Who knew how and what to study.

I know this for a fact: What we achieved as a group was *way better* than what I could ever have achieved as a law student on my own. It's kind of like the rising tide that lifts all boats. Lord knows I needed my "boat lifted" in law school. Yep, my law school study group definitely qualified as a mastermind group. In fact, I might not even be here today had I not joined one early on.

The Magic of My Attorney Mastermind Group

I run an attorney mastermind group that meets in person for two days, three times a year. This is our highest level of membership at Great Legal Marketing. Lawyers come in from all of the over the country and Canada to participate.

During these confidential meetings in which none of your competitors are allowed, member firms take turns in the hot seat to talk about what's working and what's not, and to ask others in the group for input on both. We each exchange information, share lots of our marketing materials, and deep-dive into each other's practices. It's a trusting environment, and whatever we say is kept confidential.

I've found that, in general, the marketing ideas that we bat around are all pretty interesting, though not necessarily ground-breaking or knock-your-socks-off unique. These are good market-ers. They don't use every marketing strategy but the ones they do use they use to virtual perfection. The discussions at this level tend to be more about *big* decisions: hiring and firing; buying or leasing; choosing or divorcing law partners. We also spend a fair amount of time comparing vendors, cross-referral opportunities and other opportunities outside of our group for learning. We typically bring in a guest speaker as well.

We create our own hyper-focused tribe.

GLM lawyers recognize the power of the mastermind. For us, it's a principle as much as it a practice: Surround yourself with goal-oriented people (who ideally should be smarter or more in-novative or somehow better than you) and you expand your per-spective in unimaginable ways. Plus, you really do feel less lonely.

You find your way off that desert island.

(If you're interested in joining my attorney mastermind group, which meets in the training center in my office in Fairfax, Virginia, reach out for details. While we vet new members carefully, I promise you it's worth the effort, if only because it expands your mindset and puts you in a healthier headspace altogether.)

Principles and Pizza

When I was a young lawyer starting my own practice, I started a mastermind group, I just didn't know that's what I had done at the time. Periodically, I'd invite my friends, other attorneys with whom I competed here in Fairfax, into my office and we'd order a couple of pizzas, then brainstorm, share thoughts and ideas, and talk through the challenges we were facing in our firms. Invariably, someone would say something that helped me in some way; sparked an idea, stamped out a fear, or shared a resource.

I'm still a member of a local group today. Why?

1. Because I get a lot out of it.

2. It's important that lawyers have a place to go and a resource to tap into that allows for this kind of sharing. And the fact that we have so few of these outlets doesn't make a shred of sense.

3. There are now younger lawyers in our group who benefit from the wisdom of "masters."

What Happened to All of the Mentors and Role Models?

They're still out there, but our numbers have dwindled to a dangerously low level. Where the hell did they go? What happened to them? The Internet has swallowed them up.

While I sure don't want to sound like the technology-is-killing-us guy, I still have to go there, at least for a minute, because what I'm going to say next is the sad truth: Now that we have instant (and constant) access to online communication and all the wondrous tools of the Internet, there's much less human contact, much less getting together, fewer face-to-face interactions—which used to be an important part of the mentoring process. Sad thing.

You probably know it as well as I do: There's very little organized mentoring out there for young lawyers just out of law school, the very ones who need it the most. Lots of our GLM members take on mentors in their local communities but, in general, young lawyers don't have nearly as much access to the "human" side of mentoring as we did. We need to change that. Plain and simple.

It's not just how those of us who are older mentor younger lawyers. Mentoring extends to your clients and when you do it well, you become magnetically attractive to them. Ours is not just a legal business; it's a *people* business, which means your clients need to walk away feeling satisfied with not just how you handled their case (you are expected to handle their case well) but how much you cared about their life in general; what you did (even if it was something small) to somehow improve the quality of their lives.

The more that you can actually be interested and useful in your clients' lives, the more they'll trust you and the stronger the bond will be between you and them long after their case or matter is over. We have to be *life coaches* as well as lawyers if we want to be heroes and have impact on individuals and our communities far beyond our roles as "attorneys and counselors at law."

Mentoring is an important part of the mastermind philosophy. The fact that we are stronger together than we are apart is what will (or should) lift up this entire industry.

Throughout my career, I've been very lucky with mentors. A good thing, too, because had it not been for them, I might not be where I am today, doing what I do.

I've mentioned Samy Chong several times. I like to joke that Samy's my psychologist. Every lawyer should have a Samy Chong in their lives; someone you can have an open, honest conversation with about any number of issues—whether it's about law of about life—that you just can't have with anyone else.

What I'm about to say next might not necessarily sound like a good thing, but trust me: It is good. Samy helped teach me to be selfish. His mantra is:

You cannot be selfless until you are selfish.

Meaning you have to identify what's good for you and what's good for your family, then figure out how to get it, and don't let anything get in the way of your getting it. Period.

It's kind of like the oxygen mask analogy: If your plane is going down, you put your own oxygen mask on first before helping the person beside you (even if that person is a cherished loved one). Let me put it another way: You can't take care of someone else until you can take care of yourself first.

Thank you, Samy.

Kevin Kelly is another mentor; he goes way, way back. Kevin was (and still is) an attorney in Annandale, Virginia. During my first and second years of law school, Kevin gave me my first job. He let me be the fly on the wall. I got to write pleadings and wills, follow him around the courthouse, meet other lawyers, learn how to research and try cases.

What made it even cooler was that Kevin wasn't looking for a law clerk at the time. I bugged him. I told him I would do the work for free. I just wanted "in."

To his great credit he took me up on my "offer" and allowed me to get the hands-on experience I needed, which ended up putting me on the path to a thriving, meaningful life in law. I think that's cool: That without even spending a penny, Kevin was able to offer me resources and experiences that would last a lifetime.

Thank you, Kevin.

. . .

So if you don't have a mentee, get one. Fast. We need to be doing more to lift up our young lawyers and guide them along. We need to show them our faces, not just our Facebook postings. We need to raise up the entire profession. Throughout this book I've railed against the establishment.

Soon, many of us will be "the establishment."

The continued viability of the legal profession, particularly as it relates to the solo and small firm lawyers, and today's consumer, now depends on us.

It is fitting that this last chapter focus on the power of the mastermind because I want to end with the message that we are, all of us, better together than we are apart.

This is the path that will take you towards living the life you want to live. Hundreds of your colleagues have traveled it or are considering traveling it very soon.

GLM lawyers, by virtue of the lives they lead and the principles they embrace, really do define the power of the mastermind: It's a group of like-minded individuals who've identified a goal— in this case, a thriving business, a happy home life, and a practice with principle—and the path to get you there, too.

And to start, all you need to do is—well you know already know what I'm going to say: *Start.*

So this book is going to end with the very word that defines the beginning. I did that on purpose.

Get on the path towards the life you want. Quit hesitating. Take the first step. What's the word I'm looking for?
Start.

CONCLUSION

For some, this book has likely lit a fire inside of you. "Yes, finally, someone who understands what we solo and small firm lawyers go through!" For others, maybe not so much. Maybe you hated it (in which case I doubt you are reading this conclusion anyway).

Either way is fine with me.

In his book, *Tribes,* Seth Godin says, "There is a difference between telling people what to do and *inciting a movement.* The movement happens when people talk to one another, when ideas spread within the community, and most of all, when peer support leads people to do what they always knew was the right thing."

If you like what you have read here, we have the community of solo and small firm lawyers who share and communicate ideas, support each other, and, best of all, create peer support which leads

other lawyers to live lives of significance.
Find out more at GreatLegalMarketing.com.

INDEX

A

Abiding Presence Lutheran Church, 111
accountability, 22, 77-79, 195
    partners, 208, 216, 231
adoption, 101-09, 122 (*see also* parenting)
advertising (*see* marketing)
    brand, 30, 153-54, 182
    direct response, 154, 182-84, 214
    mass, 182-83
    mistakes, 155-68
Amato, Bo, 79, 123-24
ambition (*see* entrepreneurial mentality)
Artz, Bill, 65-66
authority, 51-52, 59, 150-51 (*see also* confidence)
avatar client, 22, 176, 215, 219
Avvo™, 154, 160, 177

B

Bailey, F. Lee, 58
Bailey, Tom, 101-03
balance, 90-91, 112, 119-20, 133, 142, 171, 188-89
bar associations, 5-8, 40, 138, 140, 147, 170, 176, 185
Ben Glass Law, 80-84, 202-04, 212
Ben Glass Soccer Sportsmanship Challenge, 48
Benzinger, Ray, 64-65
billable hour, 140-41
branding, 153-54, 182-83 (*see also* advertising; marketing)
Broad, Richard, 48-49
Burns, Fraser, 51-52
business (*see* legal business)

C

D

E

F

family (*see also* adoption; parenting)
    balance, 133
    prioritizing, 3, 11, 12, 22-23, 29, 49, 74-77, 80, 92, 98, 112-13,
        120-21, 138, 203
    roles, 11, 21, 23-24, 27, 28, 30, 53, 125, 229
    time, 125-27
    well-being, 5, 7, 9, 55, 122, 236
fees, 147, 158, 166
    billable hour, 140-41
    flat-fee, 141
Forbes, Heather, 122
forever learner, 12, 49, 62-63, 82-83, 107-08, 122, 202
Foster, Tom, 41
Foster Web Marketing, 41

G

George Mason University School of Law, 61, 64-65, 98
Gerber, Michael, 89-90, 224-25
Germain, Kip, 45, 96-97
Glass, Ben, 12-13
    childhood, 19-33 (*see also* Glass family; soccer)
    children (*see* adoption; Glass, Brian; Glass, Caitlin; Glass, David;
        Glass, Emma; Glass, Kelsey; Glass, Kevin; Glass, Leah; Glass,
        Matt; Glass, Patrick; parenting)
    college, 95-98
    early career, 68-72 (*see also* entrepreneurial mentality, Shevlin &
        Glass)
    marriage (*see* Glass, Sandi)
    parents, 20, 27-32, 70-71, 99-100 (*see also* childhood)
Glass, Brian, 98-100, 107, 146
Glass, Caitlin, 101-02, 107

ABOUT THE AUTHOR

 Ben Glass is the father of nine children, four of whom are adopted from China. He is an avid youth soccer referee, an entrepreneur, and one of the world's leading experts on marketing and operating a boutique law practice. Through his attorney success organization, Great Legal Marketing, Ben has taught hundreds of solo and small firm lawyers how to market ethically and effectively using education-based, direct response style marketing.

Ben serves on the board of Love Without Boundaries, which provides healing homes and needed surgeries for orphans in developing countries, and he has run five Marine Corps Marathons on their behalf. Above all, Ben believes in the success of the solo and small firm attorney and in the power of personal responsibility.

Ben continues to practice law at his own personal injury, medical malpractice, and long-term disability firm near Washington, D.C., where he lives with his wife, Sandi.

FREE REPORTS, VIDEOS, AND MORE ARE READY FOR YOU

Would you like to see what goes into growing a solo/small law firm?

Want the latest information on online marketing, print advertisements, direct mail, broadcast ads, and more?

How about seeing "inside the mind" of how I grew and continue to grow my law firm?

I'll give you an insider's look at the process when you request my latest free offer at:

www.GreatLegalMarketing.com

Fair warning: I offer an unvarnished take on what it means to operate your law firm as a business. It doesn't always line up with the stuff you hear from the routine sources that speak to lawyers like you and me. But I promise you, it will give you both the ideas and sense of permission needed to finally grow your practice into the business you really want it to be.